EVERYDAY

Encouragement

JOURNAL

Spiritual Refreshment for Women

ISBN 978-1-60260-446-9

Published by Barbour Publishing, Inc., P.O. Box 719, Uhrichsville, Ohio 44683, www.barbourbooks.com

Our mission is to publish and distribute inspirational products offering exceptional value and biblical encouragement to the masses.

 Member of the
Evangelical Christian
Publishers Association

Printed in the United States of America.

Contents

Introduction

*May our Lord Jesus Christ himself
and God our Father. . .encourage
your hearts and strengthen you.*

2 Thessalonians 2:16–17

———

Some days we need a gentle hand to pick us up and a voice to whisper encouragement in our ears. Life can be challenging, and when trials come our way, we may feel discouraged. But God does not fail us, no matter what our days hold. His Word provides comfort for all our troubles. In these pages, we hope you will feel the touch of His tender hand and find strength for each day.

Anger

God's Plan

My dear brothers, take note of this: Everyone should be quick to listen,
slow to speak and slow to become angry.

JAMES 1:19

———

God gives good advice on anger. Often, if we listen carefully and hold our tongues, we don't become angry in the first place. Good communication forestalls a lot of emotional trauma. Hurt emotions often cause us to speak words we regret, simply making the problem worse. So when we feel tempted to become angry, let's stop, listen, and hold our tongues for a while. That's God's plan for more peaceful relationships.

_____

_____

_____

_____

_____

_____

_____

_____

_____

_____

_____

_____

_____

_____

_____

_____

_____

_____

_____

_____

_____

_____

A Prayerful Solution

I want men everywhere to lift up holy hands in prayer, without anger or disputing.

1 TIMOTHY 2:8

Anger becomes a real trap, even for Christians. When we try to settle differences angrily, we land in big trouble, affecting and even destroying a whole congregation.

One solution to anger is prayer. It's hard to stay angry with someone you pray for, even if that person continues to irritate you. As God's Spirit works in your heart, you give the other person a second, a third, or even a hundred and third chance. In Jesus, unrighteous anger cannot linger.

Letting Go of Anger

Now the works of the flesh are evident, which are: adultery. . .idolatry, sorcery, hatred, contentions, jealousies, outbursts of wrath.

GALATIANS 5:19–20 NKJV

It's not something we like to hear, but according to God, anger is right up there with sins such as adultery and idolatry.

Most of us feel wrathful occasionally. But if such feelings take hold of our lives and bitterness results, we fall into sin. When anger touches our reactions, let's use it as a warning sign of an issue that requires our attention. Through wise action and prayer, we need not let it control us.

_____

_____

_____

_____

_____

_____

_____

_____

_____

_____

_____

_____

_____

_____

_____

_____

_____

_____

_____

_____

_____

_____

_____

_____

Good Anger

Be ye angry and sin not: let not the sun go down upon your wrath.

EPHESIANS 4:26 KJV

———

We have valid reasons for anger when we see wrongdoing against the innocent. But God tells us not to let that anger last long. We need to come to Him in prayer, consider the issue in Him, and ultimately leave it in His hands. If we can help correct the wrong, we should, but letting ourselves dwell on the situation until we fume is not an option. Let anger push us to do good, not ruin our emotional health.

Gentle Speech

A gentle answer turns away wrath, but a harsh word stirs up anger.

PROVERBS 15:1

———

How you speak can strongly affect those around you. If someone is hot under the collar, do you quell that anger with calming words or inflame him with harsh ones? Do you start a forest fire with your sister who irritates you or quench the blaze with soft words?

Anger's heat makes wise decision making impossible. But God's Word offers advice that brings peace to our lives. Gentle speech leads to wiser choices.

_____

_____

_____

_____

_____

_____

_____

_____

_____

_____

_____

_____

_____

_____

_____

_____

_____

_____

_____

_____

_____

_____

_____

_____

Anxiety

In His Hands

Do not be anxious about anything, but in everything, by prayer and petition,
with thanksgiving, present your requests to God.

PHILIPPIANS 4:6

—∞—

Need a sure cure for anxiety? Start praying. As you trust that God has your best interests at heart, no matter what situation you face, His peace can replace concern. God says there's nothing you need to worry about. Just put all your troubles in His hands, and He who rules universe upon universe yet knows each hair on your head will see that everything works out right. Are you ready to trust now?

Today!

*"Therefore do not worry about tomorrow, for tomorrow will worry about itself.
Each day has enough trouble of its own."*

MATTHEW 6:34

———

You can look ahead and obsess about fears for the future or take life one day at a time and enjoy it. But you only live in today, not in the weeks, months, and years that may lie ahead. You can only change life in the moment you're in now. Since worry never improves the future and only hurts today, you'll benefit most from trusting in God and enjoying the spot where He's planted you for now.

_____

_____

_____

_____

_____

_____

_____

_____

_____

_____

_____

_____

_____

_____

_____

_____

_____

_____

_____

_____

_____

_____

_____

_____

God Is in Control

"Who of you by worrying can add a single hour to his life?"

MATTHEW 6:27

——◦◦◦——

What does worry gain us? It can't change the length of our days, except to decrease the health of our bodies. Ultimately, worry is the most self-defeating thing we can engage in. Besides, why should we give in to concern when God controls our lives? He will always set us on the right path, so we don't have to agonize over life's details.

Sharing with Jesus

Casting all your care upon him; for he careth for you.

1 Peter 5:7 KJV

———

You don't have a care in the world that you cannot share—with Jesus, that is. There isn't one thing He doesn't want to hear about from you. Before you ask a friend to pray for you (and you should do that), be certain you share your care with your best Friend, Jesus. Your human friend may try to help you and may do a lot for you, but no one helps like Jesus. There's no worry He can't alleviate or remove.

_____

_____

_____

_____

_____

_____

_____

_____

_____

_____

_____

_____

_____

_____

_____

_____

_____

_____

_____

_____

_____

_____

_____

Blessings

Blessing Others

We work hard with our own hands. When we are cursed, we bless; when we are persecuted, we endure it.

1 CORINTHIANS 4:12

———

God gave Paul many blessings, and the apostle passed them on, even if the recipients didn't seem to really deserve them. Those who cursed him (and they were, no doubt, many) did not receive a cursing in return. Instead, Paul tried to bless them. Do we follow the apostle's example? When we are cursed by the words of others, what is our response?

Powerful Prayer

"The LORD bless you and keep you; the LORD make his face shine upon you and be gracious to you."

NUMBERS 6:24–25

W ant to pray for someone? This is a good way to do it. It's the blessing God gave to Aaron and his sons to pronounce on Israel. What Christian wouldn't appreciate these words, committing her to God's care and wanting her to draw closer to Him? Who would turn down the good things God has to offer? Can you bless your friends and family with these thoughts today?

_____

_____

_____

_____

_____

_____

_____

_____

_____

_____

_____

_____

_____

_____

_____

_____

_____

_____

_____

_____

_____

_____

Living for Christ

If you live according to the sinful nature, you will die;
but if by the Spirit you put to death the misdeeds of the body, you will live.

ROMANS 8:13

Living for Christ through His Spirit offers real life, overflowing and abundant. Blessings spill over in obedient lives. But the world, at war with God, doesn't understand. Unbelievers never feel the touch of the Spirit in their hearts and lives, and Jesus' gentle love is foreign to them. Put to death worldly misdeeds, and instead of the emptiness of the world, you'll receive blessings indeed.

Hold On to Hope

The prospect of the righteous is joy, but the hopes of the wicked come to nothing.

PROVERBS 10:28

———

Trusting in Jesus gave you new life and hope for eternity. So how do you respond when life becomes dark and dull? Does hope slip away? When no obviously great spiritual works are going on, do not assume God has deserted you. Hold on to Him even more firmly and trust. He will keep His promises. Truly, what other option do you have? Without Him, hope disappears.

_____

_____

_____

_____

_____

_____

_____

_____

_____

_____

_____

_____

_____

_____

_____

_____

_____

_____

_____

_____

_____

_____

_____

An Obedient Life

How blessed are those whose way is blameless, who walk in the law of the LORD.

PSALM 119:1 NASB

Want to be blessed? Then don't live a sin-filled life. God can't pour out blessings on anyone who consistently ignores His commands. Blessings belong to those who hear God's Word and take it to heart, living it out in love. Want to be blessed? Obey the Master. You'll live blamelessly and joyfully.

Children

Share Your Faith

Train up a child in the way he should go: and when he is old, he will not depart from it.

PROVERBS 22:6 KJV

———

What a promise for Christian parents! When you feel pressured by the task, take comfort. You are not alone—your Father is with you and promises that the effective witness of your life, as you teach your children His way, will not fail to bless them.

Parents who have just come to Christ can begin the training today. It is never too late to share your faith with those you love most.

_____

_____

_____

_____

_____

_____

_____

_____

_____

_____

_____

_____

_____

_____

_____

_____

_____

_____

_____

_____

_____

_____

_____

_____

_____

A Godly Example

"Let the little children come to Me, and do not forbid them; for of such is the kingdom of heaven."

MATTHEW 19:14 NKJV

On earth, Jesus loved children. He never shut them out. Though their youth gave them little credence in Israel, He saw the faith potential in them. Certainly the children loved Jesus, too, for His kindheartedness. Do we shut children out of our lives because we are too busy or have more "important" things on our minds? Then we need to take an example from Jesus. For a new take on God's kingdom, spend time with a child today.

The Gift of Children

Sons are a heritage from the LORD, children a reward from him.

PSALM 127:3

———

Today, many people see children more as a punishment than a reward. But when you hear of parents who wish they had never had children, you know they're missing out. God creates families to love each other and share His joys. Parents who honestly live out their faith before their children can also guide them into a good family life. Are your children a blessing? God has given them as a reward, not as a punishment. Do you treat them that way?

_____

_____

_____

_____

_____

_____

_____

_____

_____

_____

_____

_____

_____

_____

_____

_____

_____

_____

_____

_____

_____

_____

_____

Wise Correction

The rod of correction imparts wisdom, but a child left to himself disgraces his mother.

PROVERBS 29:15

In today's world, fears of child abuse have caused us to ignore this verse. Have we therefore missed the power of correction, which gives our children wisdom? As God restrains us from wrongdoing, we need to stop our children, too. We need not touch a child physically to modify behavior. Will we discipline harmful actions now or lose the chance to be proud of our self-controlled children who love the Lord?

Comfort

God of Comfort

[God] comforts us in all our troubles, so that we can comfort those in any trouble with the comfort we. . .have received from God.

2 CORINTHIANS 1:4

―⦸―

When you hurt, God offers you comfort. No trouble is so large or so small that He will not help. But when you have received His strength for the trouble at hand, do you share it in turn? Comfort isn't meant to be hidden away, but passed on to those in a similar need. As part of the body of Christ, we—the church—should be sharing the knowledge that God cares for and strengthens all His children.

_____

_____

_____

_____

_____

_____

_____

_____

_____

_____

_____

_____

_____

_____

_____

_____

_____

_____

_____

_____

_____

_____

Reaching Out

Just as the sufferings of Christ flow over into our lives, so also through Christ our comfort overflows.

2 CORINTHIANS 1:5

—⟨∞⟩—

Paul knew the pain of persecution, but he also knew the deep comfort God offered. When people gave the apostle trouble, God drew His servant close to His heart. When trials come your way, God will do the same for you. If life is always going smoothly, comfort is meaningless; but when you're in the midst of trouble, He comes alongside with tender love that overflows your trials and reaches out to others.

Renewal of Faith

"As one whom his mother comforts, so I will comfort you."

ISAIAH 66:13 NKJV

—◦◦◦—

Like a tender mother, God comforts His people. When life challenges us, we have a place to renew our faith. Instead of questioning God's compassion because we face a trial, we can draw ever nearer to Him, seeking to do His will. Surrounded by His tender arms, we gain strength to go out and face the world again.

_____

_____

_____

_____

_____

_____

_____

_____

_____

_____

_____

_____

_____

_____

_____

_____

_____

_____

_____

_____

_____

_____

_____

Giver of Comfort

You ought to forgive and comfort him, so that he will not be overwhelmed by excessive sorrow.

2 CORINTHIANS 2:7

Do you know someone who is sorry for her sin? Then don't keep reminding her of it. If she has sought forgiveness and put it behind her, it is dead. Instead of criticizing, remind her of the power of God that works in her life. Encourage her when temptation calls her name. Then she will not be overcome by sorrow and fall into sin again. Give comfort, and you will be a blessing.

Contentment

God's Provision

Now godliness with contentment is great gain.

1 TIMOTHY 6:6 NKJV

———

Paul warned Timothy against false teachers who wanted to use the church for financial gain. If these people were looking for security, they were on the wrong track. Money, which comes and goes, never brings real protection. Our security lies in God's provision. Whether or not we have a large bank account, we can feel content in Jesus. The One who brought us into this world will never forget we require food, clothing, and all the rest. When we truly trust in Jesus, contentment is sure to follow.

_____

_____

_____

_____

_____

_____

_____

_____

_____

_____

_____

Look to the Shepherd

The LORD is my shepherd, I shall not be in want.

PSALM 23:1

No matter what your physical circumstances, if Jesus is your Shepherd, you never have to want spiritually. No matter what the world throws at you, you can be at peace. No fear overcomes those who follow the Shepherd as their King. He guides them through every trial, leading them faithfully into an eternity with Him.

Are you lacking contentment today? Look to the Shepherd for peace.

Watchful Love

I have learned in whatever state I am, to be content.

PHILIPPIANS 4:11 NKJV

———

Paul wasn't writing about a grit-your-teeth kind of contentment. He had learned to trust deeply in God for all his needs, so the apostle did not worry about future events. His strength lay in God, who cared for his every need, even when churches forgot him.

We, too, can be content in Jesus. If the boss doesn't give us a raise or an unexpected bill comes in, He knows it. Nothing escapes His watchful love in our lives.

_____

_____

_____

_____

_____

_____

_____

_____

_____

_____

_____

Contentment in Trouble

The fear of the LORD leads to life: Then one rests content, untouched by trouble.

PROVERBS 19:23

God doesn't promise we will never suffer trouble, but He does promise something even more important. In the middle of trouble, we will experience real life—contentment in the middle of confusion, doubt, or turmoil. Which would you prefer—trouble and life in Jesus, or trouble on its own? You can't avoid trouble here on earth. But share life with Him, and contentment will follow.

Death

"Where, O death, is your victory? Where, O death, is your sting?"

1 CORINTHIANS 15:55

Nothing in this world ameliorates the pain of death. Losing one we love reaches deep into our souls. But with His sacrifice, Jesus permanently overcame the sting of mortality. Those who trust in Him do not live for a few short years, but for eternity. When death ends their earthly lives, they simply move into heaven. When we lose loved ones, our hearts feel pain. But if they gave their lives to Jesus, He is still victorious. In time, we will meet them again in paradise.

_____

_____

_____

_____

_____

_____

_____

_____

_____

_____

_____

_____

_____

_____

_____

_____

_____

_____

_____

_____

_____

_____

_____

_____

_____

_____

Our Hope

God raised him from the dead, freeing him from the agony of death,
because it was impossible for death to keep its hold on him.

ACTS 2:24

———

Death could not grasp Jesus, the Sinless One who died for the guilty. Though it clings to sinful beings, it had no claim on God's Son. Jesus is our only hope. Though sin deserves death, God's compassion made a way to free us from its agonies. When we give our poor, mortal lives to Jesus, we rise in Him, sharing His eternal life.

Death Will Die

The last enemy to be destroyed is death.

1 CORINTHIANS 15:26

If Jesus conquered death, why do we still suffer the death of loved ones? Because today, we live in the promise of death's destruction, not its completion. God's Son has ransomed us through His sacrifice, but death still exists in our world. But one day, that will no longer be so. Jesus promises to destroy death entirely—death shall die, and heaven will be ours.

_____

_____

_____

_____

_____

_____

_____

_____

_____

_____

_____

God's Promise

This is the promise that He has promised us—eternal life.

1 JOHN 2:25 NKJV

The promise of eternal life comes straight from God. Those who receive Jesus into their hearts do not end their existence when they stop breathing. Their last breath on earth is merely a precursor of life in eternity with Jesus. Today, you miss the one you lost, and your heart aches. But in eternity, you will be reunited and will share the joys of the Savior's triumph over death. Until you meet again, simply trust in His unfailing promise.

Doubt

The Only Way

"I am the way and the truth and the life. No one comes to the Father except through me."

JOHN 14:6

—⚬—

Plenty of people doubt Jesus. But those who have accepted Him as their Savior need not wallow in uncertainty. His Spirit speaks to ours, moment by moment, if we will only listen. He tells us God has shown us the way; we need not seek another path or truth. No other road leads to God. For a vibrant Christian life, we simply need to continue down the highway we're traveling with Jesus.

_____

_____

_____

_____

_____

_____

_____

_____

_____

_____

_____

_____

_____

_____

_____

_____

_____

_____

_____

_____

_____

_____

_____

Be Faithful

Good and upright is the LORD; therefore he instructs sinners in his ways.

PSALM 25:8

—⊶⊷—

Don't know which way to turn or where to go? God will show you. Just be faithful to Him, and you will hear His still, small voice guiding you; otherwise, circumstances and wise advisers will illuminate the path you need to walk on.

Still doubting? Ask God for forgiveness for sins that bar your communion with Him. Soon, with a clean heart, you'll be headed in the right direction.

Moving Mountains

*"Whoever says to this mountain, 'Be removed and be cast into the sea,'
and does not doubt. . .but believes. . .will have whatever he says."*

MARK 11:23 NKJV

———

Don't you wish you had faith like this? Christians often try to gear up to it, willing it with all their hearts. But that's not what God had in mind. Manipulating Him cannot work.

Only when we fully trust in Him will He move our mountain—even if it's in an unexpected direction.

_____

_____

_____

_____

_____

_____

_____

_____

_____

_____

_____

_____

_____

_____

_____

_____

_____

_____

_____

_____

_____

_____

Compassion

Be merciful to those who doubt.

JUDE 1:22

If you've ever doubted (as we all have), you can understand why this verse is in the Bible. If well-meaning folks attacked you for your uncertainty, it probably didn't help—they just made you more nervous.

When questions enter our minds, we need someone encouraging to come alongside us and provide answers, not a critic who wants to condemn our feelings. Knowing that, we also need compassion for other doubters. May we be the merciful ones who aid those doubting hearts.

Eternity

Be Prepared

He has also set eternity in the hearts of men;
yet they cannot fathom what God has done from beginning to end.

ECCLESIASTES 3:11

———

Though each of us has a bit of eternity in our heart, and we cannot rest unless we know the Savior, we also cannot fathom the works of God. That can make us either dissatisfied and doubtful or relaxed, trusting children who know their Father is in control and will care for them from beginning to end. Have you trusted Him who is the Alpha and Omega? Are you prepared for eternity with Him?

_____

_____

_____

_____

_____

_____

_____

_____

_____

_____

_____

_____

_____

_____

_____

_____

_____

_____

_____

_____

_____

_____

Always Secure

Your throne was established long ago; you are from all eternity.

PSALM 93:2

——⚬⚬⚬——

There was never a moment when God did not exist. No scrap of time or eternity came into being without Him, and nothing escapes His powerful reign. That's good news for His children. For whatever we face, now or in our heavenly abode, we know our Father is in control. No spiritual warfare or earthly disaster lies beyond His plan. No wickedness of Satan can take Him by surprise. Ours is the eternal Lord, who has loved us from the start. In Him, we are always secure.

Unchanging

Your word, O Lord, is eternal; it stands firm in the heavens.

PSALM 119:89

———

The Word of God never changes. The Father's commands do not alter, and neither does Jesus, the Word made flesh, or His promise of salvation. Those who trust in Him are secure as the Lord Himself, for He does not change, and none of His promises pass away unfulfilled. The eternal Lord and all He commands stand firm. To gain eternity, simply receive Christ as your Savior; then trust in Him.

_____

_____

_____

_____

_____

_____

_____

_____

_____

_____

_____

Pure Delight

You have made known to me the path of life; you will fill me with joy in your presence,
with eternal pleasures at your right hand.

PSALM 16:11

———

Rejoicing in God? Those who do not know Jesus cannot imagine it. You have to know Jesus to delight in His presence, just as you cannot enjoy a friend until you come to know each other and enjoy companionship. But knowing and loving God brings us, His children, joy in His presence and the prospect of undefined pleasures at His side. Are you prepared to share those joys with Jesus for eternity?

Source of Salvation

He became the source of eternal salvation for all who obey him.

HEBREWS 5:9

———◦∞◦———

Salvation in Jesus is important to our earthly lives. How many times has He dispelled danger or helped us avoid it? How often has sin failed to mar our lives because we obeyed His commands? But Jesus is also the source of salvation in eternity. Instead of allowing us to remain forever in our earthly lives, God planned to bring us into everlasting life with Him in His restored kingdom. In heaven, we will praise His salvation without end.

_____

_____

_____

_____

_____

_____

_____

_____

_____

_____

_____

_____

_____

_____

_____

_____

_____

_____

_____

_____

_____

_____

Faith

Loving Jesus

Looking unto Jesus the author and finisher of our faith.

HEBREWS 12:2 KJV

Good is writing a story of faith through your life. What will it describe? Will it be a chronicle of challenges overcome, like the Old Testament story of Joseph? Or a near tragedy turned into joy, like that of the prodigal son? Whatever your account says, if you love Jesus, the end is never in question. Those who love Him finish in heaven, despite their trials on earth. The long, weary path ends in His arms. Today, write a chapter in your faithful narrative of God's love.

He Never Fails

If we are faithless, he will remain faithful, for he cannot disown himself.

2 TIMOTHY 2:13

❦

Sometimes our faith fails, but Jesus never does. When we change for the worse, slip, or make a mistake, He is still the same faithful God He's always been. Though we may falter, He cannot. If we give in to the tempter's wiles, let us turn again to the faithful One. If we have trusted in Him, we can turn to Him for renewed forgiveness. His own faithfulness will not allow Him to deny us.

_____

_____

_____

_____

_____

_____

_____

_____

_____

_____

_____

_____

_____

_____

_____

_____

_____

_____

_____

_____

_____

_____

_____

_____

Perfection

His works are perfect, and all his ways are just. A faithful God who does no wrong, upright and just is he.

DEUTERONOMY 32:4

Many unbelievers, or even weakening believers living in crisis, complain that God is unfair. But Moses, who suffered much for God's people, knew better than that. God is always perfect, faithful, and just—it's rebellious humanity that lacks these qualities.

We can have faith in God's perfection. He has never failed His people yet, though they have often been false. Trust in Him today. As He led His people to the Promised Land, He'll lead you home to Himself.

Spiritual Certainty

We live by faith, not by sight.

2 Corinthians 5:7

There is more than one way of seeing. We view the world around us with our eyes, but by doing so, we don't apprehend all there is in life. Those things we "see" by faith cannot be envisioned by our physical eyes. That's why doubters disbelieve them. But when God speaks to our hearts, it is as real as if we'd viewed the truth plainly in front of us. Like Paul, though our eyes cannot see it, we have a spiritual certainty.

_____

_____

_____

_____

_____

_____

_____

_____

_____

_____

_____

_____

_____

_____

_____

_____

_____

_____

_____

_____

_____

_____

The Christian Life

Clearly no one is justified before God by the law, because, "The righteous will live by faith."

GALATIANS 3:11

Though some might claim it, crossing all your t's and dotting your i's spiritually does not make you a great Christian. Rules and regulations aren't what the Christian life is about—faith is. Obeying God and following Him as the Spirit leads challenges you to trust Him every moment of your life. With that kind of belief, you'll share His world-changing message.

Praise Him

Let them praise the name of the LORD, for His name alone is exalted;
His glory is above the earth and heaven.

PSALM 148:13 NKJV

Trusting Jesus gives you a spectacular view of God's power. His work in your life increasingly opens your eyes to this glorious King who loves you. But those who do not know Him cannot praise Him. They are thoroughly blind to the glories of the One whom they have denied. Yet in the end, His glory will be apparent even to them. Whom do you follow—the Glorious One or mere humans?

_____

_____

_____

_____

_____

_____

_____

_____

_____

_____

_____

_____

_____

_____

_____

_____

_____

_____

_____

_____

_____

_____

_____

Our Hearts

Are you willing to recognize, you foolish fellow, that faith without works is useless?

JAMES 2:20 NASB

F aith isn't faith if actions don't follow belief. No matter what a person says, unless love, compassion, and kindness accompany her words, it would be foolish to consider her Christian testimony believable.

Though works don't save us, they show what's in our hearts. What are we proving by our works today?

Family

Shine Brightly

Each one of you also must love his wife as he loves himself, and the wife must respect her husband.

EPHESIANS 5:33

M arriage is a reciprocal relationship. For it to work well, both parties have to give and receive. If you share house space without the love and respect that make it a home, yours quickly becomes an empty existence. But that's not what God had in mind when He created marriage to reflect His own love for His people. He can help your marriage shine brightly for Him, if only you ask Him and are open to His will.

_____

_____

_____

_____

_____

_____

_____

_____

_____

_____

_____

_____

_____

_____

_____

_____

_____

_____

_____

_____

_____

_____

_____

_____

Building a House

The wise woman builds her house, but the foolish pulls it down with her hands.

PROVERBS 14:1 NKJV

Did you know you can build a house? God says so. No, you won't use mortar, brick, and wood. But every Christian woman has the ability to build up her family with her wisdom, industry, and righteousness. Her faithful Christian character blesses those in her home. Today, are you building your house or tearing it down? Seek God, and He will help you make it strong.

Parents

"Honor your father and your mother, that your days may be long upon the land."

EXODUS 20:12 NKJV

When we honor our parents, we may not spend much time in the Promised Land, but God will bless us. Treating Mom and Dad well improves our relationships with them and gives our family security. As we treat our children's grandparents well, we model the actions of adult children, and our children are more likely to treat us well, too.

Our Father God has special blessings for those of us who respect our parents. Whether it's Holy Land property or deeper love, He gives us just what we need.

_____

_____

_____

_____

_____

_____

_____

_____

_____

_____

_____

_____

_____

Appreciation for Mothers

Her children arise and call her blessed; her husband also, and he praises her.

PROVERBS 31:28

—◦◦◦◦—

Wouldn't every woman like to receive this kind of praise? A few do. Yet, though we all need praise for a job well done, many families forget to encourage their members. When we have followed God faithfully, it shows in our lives, but we still value others' appreciation. Has a Christian mother been a wonderful influence on your life? She'd probably like to know that. Feel free to share that praise with others, too.

Fear

Fear Will Flee

*Do not be afraid of sudden terror, nor of trouble from the wicked when it comes;
for the Lord will be your confidence, and will keep your foot from being caught.*

PROVERBS 3:25–26 NKJV

What do you have to fear, with God as your confidence? He protects you from being snared like a wild animal by the world's troubles. With His hand over you, no sudden event or evildoer's plot can destroy you. Give Him your confidence, and fear will flee.

_____

_____

_____

_____

_____

_____

_____

_____

_____

_____

_____

_____

_____

_____

_____

_____

_____

_____

_____

_____

_____

_____

Fearing God

In the fear of the Lord there is strong confidence, and His children will have a place of refuge.

Proverbs 14:26 NKJV

⬥

There is only one right kind of fear—the fear of God. Not that we need to cower before Him, but we must respect and honor Him and His infinite power. Those who love Him also rightly fear Him. But those who fear God need fear nothing else. He is their refuge, the Protector whom nothing can bypass. Fear God, and you are safe.

Whom Do You Fear?

"I tell you, my friends, do not be afraid of those who kill the body and after that can do no more."

LUKE 12:4

Whom do you fear? If it's anyone other than God, take heart. You need not concern yourself with anything that person can do to you. Even those who can take your life can't change your eternal destination. So if someone doesn't like your faith, don't sweat it. Put your trust in God and serve Him faithfully, and you need not fear.

_____

_____

_____

_____

_____

_____

_____

_____

_____

_____

_____

_____

_____

_____

_____

_____

_____

_____

_____

_____

_____

_____

_____

Freedom from Fear

You came near when I called you, and you said, "Do not fear."

LAMENTATIONS 3:57

As tentacles of fear attempt to wrap themselves about us, we struggle to escape. But freedom lies in our Redeemer. His still, small voice speaks to our hearts: "Do not fear. What terror is greater than I am?"

He who created the universe will never be taken unaware by troubles or disturbed by our dread. They cannot disrupt His plan. The future lies clear before His eyes, and He saves us from every harm.

Secure in the Father

For you did not receive a spirit that makes you a slave again to fear, but you received the Spirit of sonship. And by him we cry, "Abba, Father."

ROMANS 8:15

As part of God's family, you need never dread anything. He who rules the universe adopted you. Since your loving Father no longer condemns you for sin, panic need not rule your life. Fear no retribution, because your elder brother Jesus shed His blood for you, covering every sin. God's child always remains secure in her Abba, "Daddy."

_____

_____

_____

_____

_____

_____

_____

_____

_____

_____

_____

_____

_____

_____

_____

_____

_____

_____

_____

_____

_____

_____

_____

Forgiveness

Blessing of Forgiveness

[Our] sins have been forgiven on account of his name.

1 JOHN 2:12

Who could do something wonderful enough to earn God's forgiveness? No human work can buy it. God forgives because of who He is, not because of who we are or what we do. That's encouraging, because we can't earn forgiveness by our own perfection. Instead, forgiveness becomes the great blessing of our Christian life that makes living for Jesus possible. We obey God to show our appreciation, not to gain entry into His kingdom.

An End to Mourning

"Blessed are those who mourn, for they will be comforted."

MATTHEW 5:4

How often do we think of mourning as a good thing? But when it comes to sin, it is. Those who sorrow over their own sinfulness will turn to God for forgiveness. When He willingly responds to their repentance, mourning ends. Comforted by God's pardon, transformed sinners celebrate— and joyous love for Jesus replaces sorrow.

_____

_____

_____

_____

_____

_____

_____

_____

_____

_____

_____

_____

_____

_____

_____

_____

_____

_____

_____

_____

_____

_____

The Price of Forgiveness

And according to the law almost all things are purified with blood,
and without shedding of blood there is no remission.

HEBREWS 9:22 NKJV

Many people in our world would like cheap forgiveness. They want someone to say they are okay, but they don't want to pay any price for their wrongdoing. That's not what the scriptures say. Remission of sins comes at a high price—sacrificial blood, the blood of Jesus. Jesus says you are worth this expense, and you are clean in Him. Put sin away and rejoice in His deep love for you.

Pass It On

"If you forgive others for their transgressions, your heavenly Father will also forgive you."

MATTHEW 6:14, NASB

———

Forgiveness isn't only something God gives us. He designed it to be passed on to others. Doing that, we learn the value of the pardon the Father has offered us. Even when everything in us screams, "No, I can't forgive," He empowers us to do so, if we trust in Him. Our loving Father never commands us to do anything He cannot also strengthen us to do.

_____

_____

_____

_____

_____

_____

_____

_____

_____

_____

_____

_____

_____

_____

_____

_____

_____

_____

_____

_____

_____

_____

_____

_____

_____

Friendship

Chosen Family

There is a friend that sticketh closer than a brother.

PROVERBS 18:24 KJV

Family relationships range from the wonderful to the disturbing, and we get whatever God gives us. But we choose our friends based on common interests and experiences. Often this "chosen family" seems closer to us than siblings. Yet neither clings closer than our elder brother Jesus. He teaches us how to love blood relatives and those we choose. No matter whether or not we're related, when we love in Him, that love sticks fast.

Disconnect from the World

Whosoever therefore will be a friend of the world is the enemy of God.

JAMES 4:4 KJV

———

There are good friendships and bad ones. When Christ becomes your best friend, other relationships may become distant. Old, carnal friendships no longer seem so attractive. Your lifestyles clash, and old friends become confused. But this separation is part of God's plan of holiness. Jesus disconnects you from the world and draws you close to His people—Christian friends who share your love for Him. Together, you may reach out to those old friends for Jesus, too.

_____

_____

_____

_____

_____

_____

_____

_____

_____

_____

_____

_____

_____

_____

_____

_____

_____

_____

_____

_____

_____

_____

_____

Importance of Friendship

Do not forsake your friend and the friend of your father, and do not go to your brother's house when disaster strikes you—better a neighbor nearby than a brother far away.

PROVERBS 27:10

Friendship is important to God, or He would not encourage us to hold fast to it. As Christians, we've known times when other believers seemed closer than our kin. God has brought us into a new family—His own—where faith becomes more important than blood. Through Him, our love expands, and we help each other when trouble strikes. No matter where you go, God's people are near.

Our Best Friend

A righteous man is cautious in friendship, but the way of the wicked leads them astray.

PROVERBS 12:26

———∞∞∞———

We need friends. But there are those who will lead us into trouble and those who will encourage us and lift us up in our faith, drawing us ever nearer to God. Before we draw near to others, do we consider their spiritual impact on us? If God is our best friend, let us be cautious not to be led astray. When we share friendship with Jesus and our earthly friends, we are truly blessed.

_____

_____

_____

_____

_____

_____

_____

_____

_____

_____

_____

_____

Giving

Prayerful Giving

Give, and it shall be given unto you; good measure, pressed down. . .and running over.

LUKE 6:38 KJV

Need an example of how to give? Look to God. To those who give generously, He gives over-flowing, abundant blessings.

In this fallen world, we need to be careful to whom we give support. Dishonest people or those who oppose God should not be our charitable choices. But many Christian ministries do good work and need our support. Faithful churches need our giving. As we donate prayerfully, God will bless us in return.

Want versus Need

"Give us this day our daily bread."

MATTHEW 6:11 NKJV

———

Jesus tells us here to ask God for our daily needs, and we may do that frequently. Let's remember that even the smallest things, such as the bread we put on the table, come from God. Yet have we forgotten that all our food comes from our heavenly Father? God forgets nothing we need. So if we don't have steak instead of hamburgers, could it be because we want, but don't need, it?

_____

_____

_____

_____

_____

_____

_____

_____

_____

_____

_____

_____

_____

_____

_____

_____

_____

_____

_____

_____

_____

_____

_____

Share His Love

"It is more blessed to give than to receive."

Acts 20:35

Christmas has become a time of receiving—to the point where greed motivates more people than blessing. But Paul reminds us that getting what we want is not the greatest blessing. We know this when we see the delight in a child's eyes at receiving a longed-for item. Our heavenly Father loves to see the same joy in our eyes when He helps us in less tangible ways. That's why He tells us to share His love with others.

Getting What You Give

Whoever sows sparingly will also reap sparingly,
and whoever sows generously will also reap generously.

2 CORINTHIANS 9:6

W hat you give is what you get. That's true in life, and it's also true spiritually. Those who try to hold their finances close will be letting go of spiritual blessings, while those who share generously gain in countless ways. It's hard to give up worldly treasures, but when you give in the name of Jesus, you will never run short.

_____

_____

_____

_____

_____

_____

_____

_____

_____

_____

_____

_____

God as Father

Loving Correction

For whom the LORD loves He corrects, just as a father the son in whom he delights.

PROVERBS 3:12 NKJV

———

Do you feel the pain of God's correction? Take heart, since it shows He loves you. Just as a loving father will not let his child walk in a dangerous place, your heavenly Father is redirecting you onto another path. Today's discipline may hurt, but in days to come, your sorrow will turn to joy as you reap the blessing that follows obedience. Your Father loves you deeply.

Compassion

A father to the fatherless, a defender of widows, is God in his holy dwelling.

PSALM 68:5

———◆———

God's love is very tender toward those who hurt. Children who have lost their fathers and women who have lost their husbands can count on His compassion. When we lose a loved one, do we focus on the Father's gentleness? We are more likely to complain that He did not extend life than to praise Him for His care. But when we feel the most pain, we also receive the largest portion of God's comfort. What hurts His children hurts Him, too.

_____

_____

_____

_____

_____

_____

_____

_____

_____

_____

_____

_____

_____

_____

_____

_____

_____

_____

_____

_____

_____

_____

_____

Heavenly Father

The mighty God, The everlasting Father.

ISAIAH 9:6 KJV

———

If you have accepted Jesus as your Savior, God is always your Father. Distance, disagreement, or death cannot change that, though each may separate you from your earthly father. But a human parent is neither mighty nor everlasting and may fail physically or spiritually. Only your heavenly Father will always be there for you, guiding you every step of the way. When you need help, call on your Father; He will never fail.

Children of God

Because you are sons, God sent the Spirit of his Son into our hearts,
the Spirit who calls out, "Abba, Father."

GALATIANS 4:6

———

God draws His children near, connecting them firmly to Himself through the Son and the Holy Spirit. There is no division in the Godhead when it comes to loving God's adopted children. With the Spirit, we call out, "Abba, Daddy," to the Holy One who loved us enough to call us to Himself, despite our sin. Through Jesus' sacrifice and the Spirit's work, God the Father cleanses us and opens the line of communication so we can follow Him truly.

_____

_____

_____

_____

_____

_____

_____

_____

_____

_____

_____

_____

_____

_____

_____

_____

_____

_____

_____

_____

_____

He Loves You This Much!

How great is the love the Father has lavished on us, that we should be called children of God! And that is what we are!

1 JOHN 3:1

God does not give His love in dribs and drabs. He lavishes it on us when we come to Him in faith. All along, He was waiting to make us His children, and we were the ones who resisted. But once we face Him as His children, God's love lets loose in our lives. Nothing is too good for His obedient children. Praise God that He loves you that much!

Turn to Him

"I will be a Father to you, and you shall be My sons and daughters, says the Lord Almighty."

2 CORINTHIANS 6:18 NKJV

———

Only unconfessed sin can separate you from the Father. But God never desires such distance. He wants to draw near, like a loving Father who holds His child, provides for her, and helps her at every turn.

Though your earthly father was less than perfect, your heavenly Father is not. He heals your hurts, solves your problems, and offers His love at every turn. All you need to do is turn to Him in love.

_____

_____

_____

_____

_____

_____

_____

_____

_____

_____

_____

God as Refuge

Stand Firm

The LORD has become my fortress, and my God the rock in whom I take refuge.

PSALM 94:22

Are you under attack by friends, family, or coworkers? If harassment comes because of your obedience to the Lord, stand firm in the face of their comments. He will defend you. If you face harsh words or nasty attitudes, remain kind, and He will assist you. Should your boss do you wrong, don't worry. Those who are against a faithful Christian are also against God, and He will somehow make things right.

Our Refuge

The LORD Almighty is the one you are to regard as holy. . .and he will be a sanctuary.

ISAIAH 8:13–14

When you live in awe of God—when He alone is Lord of your life—you have nothing to fear. If fears or enemies assail you, a place of refuge is always nearby. God never throws His children to the wolves. Instead, He protects them in His holy place. With Jesus as your Savior, you always have a peaceful place to go.

_____

_____

_____

_____

_____

_____

_____

_____

_____

_____

_____

_____

Receive His Strength

The Lord also will be a refuge for the oppressed, a refuge in times of trouble.

PSALM 9:9 NKJV

The Psalms often speak of God as a refuge. Whether you face something large, like oppression, or something much smaller, He wants you to turn to Him in troublous times. Size does not matter, but your trust in Jesus does. Nothing you face is a shock to Him—He knows your troubles and has not deserted you. So go to your refuge and take strength from Him.

Nothing Is Hidden

Nothing in all creation is hidden from God's sight.

Hebrews 4:13

———

Good or bad, nothing escapes God's notice. None of it is unknown to the Creator of the universe. And because He knows all, we can completely trust in Him. He protects us from the wicked and supports the good in our lives, because He knows just how both will touch us. When sorrow or trouble comes our way, we can count on His using it to benefit us—here and in eternity.

———————————————————————————————

———————————————————————————————

———————————————————————————————

———————————————————————————————

———————————————————————————————

———————————————————————————————

———————————————————————————————

———————————————————————————————

———————————————————————————————

———————————————————————————————

———————————————————————————————

_____

_____

_____

_____

_____

_____

_____

_____

_____

_____

_____

_____

God's Faithfulness

Always Faithful

I will never leave thee, nor forsake thee.

HEBREWS 13:5 KJV

Even when fear or stress challenges you, you need never deal with it single-handedly if Jesus rules your life. When your life seems in shambles around you, He offers strength and comfort for a hurting heart. God never gives up on you. His love cannot change. Today, delight in the One who never deserts you.

Nothing Is Impossible

"For nothing is impossible with God."

LUKE 1:37

The angel spoke these words to Mary as he gave her the news that the aged Elizabeth would bear a child. God deals with the impossible in our lives, too. We do not bear a Savior, but how has He helped us understand impossible relationships, juggle a hectic schedule, or help a hurting friend? God offers aid, whatever we face. Nothing is impossible for the One at work in our lives. What impossibilities can He deal with in your life? Have you trusted Him for help?

_____

_____

_____

_____

_____

_____

_____

_____

_____

_____

_____

_____

_____

_____

_____

_____

_____

_____

_____

_____

_____

_____

_____

_____

He Is Faithful

Blessed is he whose help is the God of Jacob. . .the LORD, who remains faithful forever.

PSALM 146:5–6

You are not the only one who has experienced God's faithfulness. Through the years, believers have experienced His provision. Read Old Testament accounts of those who have never seen Him fail. Watch His acts in the New Testament as He showed the church that it could trust Him. God cannot fail His children, and He will not fail you. Trust in the God of Jacob, and pass on your testimony of His faithfulness.

God Offers Hope

*"For I know the plans I have for you," declares the LORD, "plans to prosper you
and not to harm you, plans to give you hope and a future."*

JEREMIAH 29:11

As Judah headed into exile, conquered by a savage pagan people, God offered them hope. He still had a good plan for them, one that would come out of suffering. Their prosperity was not at an end, though their path through hardship had begun.

When God leads you up a rocky path, your hope and future remain secure in Him. Faithful trust is all He asks of you.

_____

_____

_____

_____

_____

_____

_____

_____

_____

_____

_____

_____

_____

_____

_____

_____

_____

_____

_____

_____

_____

_____

_____

_____

God's Help

Call on Him

Our help is in the name of the Lord, the Maker of heaven and earth.

Psalm 124:8

———❦———

The name God told to Moses, "I am who I am," describes His unchanging nature. So here, when the Unchanging One promises to help us, that assurance never alters. What in heaven or on earth could be too powerful or too much trouble for its Maker? Nothing is greater than God, not even our biggest challenge. We need only call His name.

All-Powerful

God is our refuge and strength, an ever-present help in trouble.

PSALM 46:1

———

When we face serious troubles, people often cannot provide the solution. Limited by human frailty, even the most generous of them can only help us so much. In every trouble, we have a greater asset, if we believe in Jesus. Our all-powerful Creator offers protection from harm and strength for the longest trial. He always wants to come to our aid. Facing a trouble of any size? Turn to Him today.

_____

_____

_____

_____

_____

_____

_____

_____

_____

_____

_____

_____

_____

Never Forgotten

Who is like the LORD our God. . .who stoops down to look on the heavens and the earth?

PSALM 113:5–6

———

This all-powerful Lord, to whom the heavens and earth are small, cares not just for your universe, but for you. The verses that follow these describe His love for even the humblest person. Though you may face times of struggle, your awesome Lord will never forget you. One day, as verse 8 of this psalm promises, even the humble can sit with princes.

Ask for Help

Let us then approach the throne of grace with confidence,
so that we may receive mercy and find grace to help us in our time of need.

HEBREWS 4:16

Don't feel shy about approaching Jesus with all your cares. As God's child, you have a special place in His heart. When you have failed, you need not fear coming to the King of kings for mercy and grace. He is just waiting for you to admit the problem and ask for help. Seek Jesus' aid, whatever your trouble. That's what He wants you to do.

_____

_____

_____

_____

_____

_____

_____

_____

_____

_____

_____

_____

_____

_____

_____

_____

_____

_____

_____

_____

_____

_____

Purposeful Plan

And we know that all things work together for good to those who love God,
to those who are the called according to His purpose.

ROMANS 8:28 NKJV

Life doesn't always look ideal to us. When finances are tight, family problems are serious, or things just don't seem to go our way, we may doubt that God is working in our lives. That's the time we need to reread this verse and take heart. Even things that don't seem good have a purpose in God's plan. As Christians, we can trust in Him, even when life is less than perfect.

God's Love

Open Door

*"For God so loved the world that he gave his one and only Son,
that whoever believes in him shall not perish but have eternal life."*

JOHN 3:16

These words are God's open door to those who believe in His Son. The barrier between God's holiness and man's sinfulness disintegrates when we believe in Jesus' sacrifice for human sin. But we must walk through that open door, with faith, to inherit the eternal life God offers. Have you taken that step, or are you still outside the door?

_____

_____

_____

_____

_____

_____

_____

_____

_____

_____

_____

_____

_____

_____

_____

_____

_____

_____

_____

_____

_____

Tender Love

*This is love: not that we loved God, but thathe loved us
and sent his Son as an atoning sacrifice for our sins.*

1 JOHN 4:10

W e weren't sitting around thinking about loving God before He touched our lives. God began the process before we were even born. He sent His Son to bring us into communion with Him, and His Spirit drew us into a relationship with Him. We respond to God's overwhelmingly tender love when we invite Jesus into our lives. Even so, many years of obedience show our gratitude, but they never repay His loving compassion.

Gift of Love

The LORD takes delight in his people.

PSALM 149:4

God doesn't just like you—He delights in you. You are very special to Him; He brought you into His salvation so He could spend eternity with you. God loves each of His children in a special way. You aren't just another in a long line of His people. He knows every bit of you, your faithfulness and failures, and loves each part of you "to pieces." We could never earn such love—it is His special gift to each of us. Let's rejoice in that blessing today.

_____

_____

_____

_____

_____

_____

_____

_____

_____

_____

_____

_____

God's Love Is at Work

We have known and believed the love that God has for us. God is love,
and he who abides in love abides in God, and God in him.

1 JOHN 4:16 NKJV

———✦———

Trusting in Jesus, you have felt God's love at work in your inner being. The vibrant connection that only Christians experience becomes the center of your life. If you are faithful, His eternal life renews you from head to toe and shines forth vibrantly. Your Spirit-inspired words and actions truly portray God's love to the world.

By Your Side

Love is patient, love is kind. It does not envy, it does not boast, it is not proud.

1 CORINTHIANS 13:4

———

God's love is not short-tempered or short-lived. Unlike human love, it never gives up on you, even on those long, discouraging days when your job is a strain, family life becomes confused, and you hardly know where to turn. In such stressful times, your heavenly Father puts up with all of it, right beside you. He's not out there somewhere—He's close by your side.

God's Mercy

Appreciation for Mercy

The L<small>ORD</small> your God is a merciful God; he will not abandon or destroy you.

D<small>EUTERONOMY</small> 4:31

E<small>ven</small> when we fail God, He does not fail us. He knows our frailty and has mercy when we come to Him seeking forgiveness and wanting to change our ways. Mercy never holds grudges or seeks revenge, but it wants the best for forgiven sinners. So our merciful Lord calls us to make changes that show we appreciate what He has done for us. Is some appreciation called for in your life?

Endurance

As you know, we consider blessed those who have persevered. You have heard of Job's perseverance and have seen what the Lord finally brought about. The Lord is full of compassion and mercy.

JAMES 5:11

———

Endurance in faith, hard as it may seem, brings happiness. Trials are not a sign of God's disfavor or His will to carelessly punish His children. The tenderhearted Savior never acts cruelly. But through troubles, we draw close to Him and see God's power at work in our lives. Then, as with Job, when we persevere in faith, God rewards us bountifully.

_____

_____

_____

_____

_____

_____

_____

_____

_____

_____

_____

_____

_____

_____

_____

_____

_____

_____

_____

_____

_____

_____

_____

_____

Mercy Triumphs

Mercy triumphs over judgment!

James 2:13

———

Not only is God merciful to us, but He expects us to pass that blessing on to others. Instead of becoming the rule enforcers in this world, we are called to paint a picture of the tender love He has for fallen people and to call many other sinners into His love. When we criticize the world and do not show compassion, we lose the powerful witness we were meant to have. As you stand firm for Jesus, may mercy also triumph in your life.

Rebirth and Renewal

He saved us, not because of righteous things we had done, but because of his mercy.
He saved us through the washing of rebirth and renewal by the Holy Spirit.

TITUS 3:5

Could we save ourselves? No way! Even our best efforts fall far short of God's perfection. If God had left us on our own, we'd be eternally separated from Him. But graciously, the Father reached down to us through His Son, sacrificing Jesus on the cross. Then the Spirit touched our lives in rebirth and renewal. Together, the three Persons of the Godhead saved us in merciful love.

_____

_____

_____

_____

_____

_____

_____

_____

_____

_____

_____

_____

Joy in Our Troubles

Great is your love, reaching to the heavens; your faithfulness reaches to the skies.

PSALM 57:10

H as God's mercy touched your life so deeply that you want to shout His praises to the skies? That's how the psalmist felt as he trusted in God despite his troubles. When we look to God in our troubles, our burdened hearts can still find joy. Though we are small and weak, He is most powerful. His strength will overcome our deepest problems, if only we let it.

Overflowing Mercy

*O Israel, put your hope in the LORD, for with the LORD is unfailing love
and with him is full redemption.*

PSALM 130:7

Why hope in God, even in dire situations? Because every one of His people greatly needs His overflowing mercy. Our lives are frail, but He is not. Jesus brings the redemption we require. No matter what we face, Jesus walks with us. We need only trust faithfully that His salvation is on the way.

God's Provision

God Meets Our Needs

*"He has brought down rulers from their thrones but has lifted up the humble.
He has filled the hungry with good things but has sent the rich away empty."*

<small>LUKE 1:52–53</small>

God provides for every one of His children, even the humblest. Wealth cannot gain His favor nor poverty destroy it. The Father does not look at the pocketbook, but at the heart. Those who love Him, though they may lack cash, see their needs fulfilled, but unbelievers who own overflowing storehouses harvest empty hearts. God never ignores His children's needs. What has He given you today?

He Will Never Fail

You open your hand and satisfy the desires of every living thing.

PSALM 145:16

—⦿—

Our faithful Lord provides for all His created beings. Will He fail to care for you? How could He satisfy the needs of the smallest birds and beasts, yet forget His human child? God is always faithful. Though we fail, He will not. He cannot forget His promises of love and will never forget to provide for your every need.

_____

_____

_____

_____

_____

_____

_____

_____

_____

_____

_____

His Gifts

If, by the trespass of the one man, death reigned through that one man,
how much more will those who receive God's abundant provision of grace
and of the gift of righteousness reign in life through the one man, Jesus Christ.

ROMANS 5:17

———

What greater gift could God give us than His grace? Once, death ruled over us. Now, life in Christ commands our days. As we ponder God's compassion, do we appreciate Christ's sacrifice? Any spiritual value we have comes from His gifts. We can never repay Him, but are we living to show how much we care?

Trust God

Abraham answered, "God himself will provide the lamb for the burnt offering, my son."

Genesis 22:8

—∞∞—

Though God had commanded Abraham to sacrifice his son Isaac, the patriarch had faith his son would not die. All it took was a ram caught in a bush. Because of Abraham's faith, the sheep was just where he needed it at the right moment. God provided just what was necessary—a sacrifice and a living son. Do you need God's provision today? Trust the God who made a way for Abraham to make a way for you, too.

_____

_____

_____

_____

_____

_____

_____

_____

_____

_____

_____

_____

_____

_____

_____

_____

_____

_____

_____

_____

_____

Let His Light Shine

For Christ's sake, I delight in weaknesses, in insults, in hardships, in persecutions, in difficulties.
For when I am weak, then I am strong.

2 CORINTHIANS 12:10

Only God can make you strong in the weak places. In those spots of persecution and hardship, His power and grace shine through your fragile vessel as you live as a faithful Christian. When you feel broken and useless, trust in Him to fill your flaws, and His light will shine through the cracks of your pain and reach a hurting world.

God's Word

The Living Word

The word of God is living and active and sharper than any two-edged sword,
and piercing as far as the division of soul and spirit.

HEBREWS 4:12 NASB

The Bible is not a dead book. The writer of Hebrews says it lives; and those who trust in Jesus can attest to this truth. Have you read a scripture and felt God knew just what you required, because it related to your needs in a special way? Then you've experienced the living Word of God that pierces your soul and spirit. Live by it in His love.

_____

_____

_____

_____

_____

_____

_____

_____

_____

_____

_____

_____

_____

_____

_____

_____

_____

_____

_____

_____

_____

_____

Knowing God

In the beginning was the Word, and the Word was with God, and the Word was God.

JOHN 1:1

Want a picture of God's Word? Look at Jesus, the embodiment of everything the Father wanted to say to us. You can't do that if you don't read the Book that tells of Him.

Maybe that's why God takes it personally when we decide not to read His Word. We're ignoring His tender commands and pushing aside His love. God's scriptures communicate with His children. How can we know Him without His Word?

Flawless Words

"Every word of God is flawless."

PROVERBS 30:5

———

Maybe you've had days when you've been tempted to doubt this verse. You wanted to go in one direction, and God's Word said to go in another. But if you were wise, you trusted in its truth instead of following your own way. After all, can you claim that your every word is error free? No. How much better to follow in the perfect way of your Lord, who willingly shares His wisdom. To avoid many of the faults of this world, trust the flawless Word of God.

_____

_____

_____

_____

_____

_____

_____

_____

_____

_____

_____

_____

_____

_____

_____

_____

_____

_____

_____

_____

_____

_____

_____

Commitment and Action

Now by this we know that we know Him, if we keep His commandments.

1 JOHN 2:3 NKJV

————⦵⦵⦵————

How do you know you are a Christian? By the way you follow your Lord's commandments. Salvation is not just a matter of feeling His touch in your life. Faith is not simply a matter of emotion; it requires commitment and action, too. Real love for God includes a passion for following Him. Love Him, and your life will serve Him, too.

Living Consistently

Then Jesus said to those Jews who believed Him,
"If you abide in My word, you are My disciples indeed."

JOHN 8:31 NKJV

———

Here, Jesus talks to His disciples about a habitual lifestyle. He wanted them to live consistently in the truth He had taught them, not pull His Word out once a week or live by it once in a while. But this verse isn't only for those who walked with Jesus during His earthly ministry. Today, His Spirit helps us live consistently for Him. As we connect with the scriptures and obey His commands, we become disciples, too.

_____

_____

_____

_____

_____

_____

_____

_____

_____

_____

_____

_____

Guidance

Safe in His Will

Your hand will guide me, your right hand will hold me fast.

PSALM 139:10

Need to make a life-changing decision? God wants to be part of it. As the psalmist understood, allowing Him to guide your steps means you won't get off track and land in a nasty situation. For the believer, the best place to be is in the palm of God's hand, safe from harm and in the center of His will.

Every Step of the Way

He will be our guide even to the end.

PSALM 48:14

———

When we are facing dire troubles, God never deserts us. As life ebbs away, He does not step back from our need. No, the Eternal One guides us every step of the way, whether life is joyous or discouraging. God never gives up on you and never fails you. So don't give up on yourself. When times are hard, grab onto Him more firmly. He will never leave you nor forsake you. And in the end, you will step into His arms in heaven.

_____

_____

_____

_____

_____

_____

_____

_____

_____

_____

_____

_____

_____

_____

_____

_____

_____

_____

_____

_____

_____

_____

_____

You Can't Go Wrong

"In your unfailing love you will lead the people you have redeemed.
In your strength you will guide them to your holy dwelling."

EXODUS 15:13

———◦⊛◦———

By following Jesus, you always head in the right direction. Though the way may seem dark or convoluted, and you may often wonder if you're on the right track, as His Spirit leads you, you cannot go wrong. Your powerful Lord directs you in His everlasting way. If you start to go astray, He will guide your steps. God's love never deserts His obedient child.

The Light

When Jesus spoke again to the people, he said, "I am the light of the world.
Whoever follows me will never walk in darkness, but will have the light of life."

JOHN 8:12

Following the light of the world means you can see where you're headed. Even when life becomes confusing and totally dark, your goal hasn't changed, and you keep heading in the right direction. Walking in Jesus' light, though you hit a dark patch, you remain on the road with the Savior, and in Him you always see enough to take the next step.

_____

_____

_____

_____

_____

_____

_____

_____

_____

_____

_____

_____

Hope

Hope in Him

Put your hope in God, for I will yet praise him, my Savior and my God.

PSALM 42:5–6

———

W here else should the believer place her hope? No human has power to turn her life around without Jesus. No solution lies beyond Him, and He never pushes her away. When the world becomes harsh, she still receives His gentle encouragement.

Though you wait long and the path seems hard, hold on to Jesus. Words of praise will pass your lips as you see His salvation accomplished. Your God will never let you fall.

Overflow with Hope

May the God of hope fill you with all joy and peace as you trust in him,
so that you may overflow with hope by the power of the Holy Spirit.

ROMANS 15:13

———

Where does hope come from? From God. Unbelievers may have moments of wishful thinking or snatches of optimism in their lives, but they cannot exist in an abiding hope. Christians, filled with the Spirit, see hope overflow as they live in Christ, fulfilling the will of the Father.

Have faith? Then you have every reason to hope each day.

_____

_____

_____

_____

_____

_____

_____

_____

_____

_____

_____

_____

_____

_____

_____

_____

_____

_____

_____

_____

_____

_____

_____

Be Strong

Be strong and take heart, all you who hope in the Lord.

PSALM 31:24

Hope is not some weak, airy-fairy kind of thing. It takes strength to put your trust in God when life batters your heart and soul. Weaklings rarely hold on to positive expectation for long, because it takes too much from them. But the spiritually strong put their trust in God and let Him lift up their hearts in hope. Then battering may come, but it cannot destroy them. Hope makes Christians stronger still.

Unfailing Love

The Lord delights in those who. . .put their hope in his unfailing love.

PSALM 147:11

———— ❧ ————

We can hope in a lot of things that fail us miserably, or we can enjoy a blind optimism that leads us into trouble. But when we hope in God, who has loved us completely, our faith cannot fail. Could the One who delights in our trust forget to bless our anticipation of an eternity with Him?

Make God joyful today as you put your trust in His everlasting love.

_____

_____

_____

_____

_____

_____

_____

_____

_____

_____

_____

_____

_____

_____

_____

_____

_____

_____

_____

_____

_____

_____

_____

_____

Prosperity Returns

"Then I will make up to you for the years that the swarming locust has eaten."

JOEL 2:25 NASB

———❦———

Those of us who rejoice in God can trust that even though the consuming locusts of life destroy our blessings, God will replace them. Though hardship makes us struggle awhile, God turns the situation around and pours out blessings on His faithful people. Prosperity returns to those who love Him well, if we determinedly love Him. In heaven or on earth, the blessing appears again.

Where Is Your Hope?

Find rest, O my soul, in God alone; my hope comes from him.

PSALM 62:5

⸺⸳⸻

Those who hope in worldly things are destined for frustration and disappointment, but Christians rest in God, so instead of frustration, they receive blessing and confidence from their powerful Savior.

Where is your hope today? If it's in things, you are bound to worry, but hope in God is always fulfilled. Relax in the knowledge that He never fails.

_____

_____

_____

_____

_____

_____

_____

_____

_____

_____

_____

_____

_____

_____

_____

_____

_____

_____

_____

_____

_____

_____

_____

Joy

Obedience = Joy

"I have told you this so that my joy may be in you and that your joy may be complete."

JOHN 15:11

What wouldn't we do to share Jesus' complete joy! But this verse comes after one of Jesus' commands to obedience. Ah, now do we change our minds? Does joy suddenly become impossible? When Jesus calls us to act, do we follow, or do we decide it's too hard and give up immediately? Let's keep our eyes on the outcome—the joy of our Lord filling our lives. Then obedience, too, may become a joy.

Joy Will Come

My lips will shout for joy when I sing praise to you—I, whom you have redeemed.

PSALM 71:23

———⊗⊗⊗———

Having trouble finding joy in your life today? Do what the psalmists often did and remind yourself what God has already done for you. How many ways has following Him blessed you? Begin by thanking Him for His saving grace, and the joy starts, no matter what you face today. Your lips will show the delight in your heart.

_____

_____

_____

_____

_____

_____

_____

_____

_____

_____

_____

_____

_____

_____

_____

_____

_____

_____

_____

_____

_____

_____

_____

Sorrow to Joy

"I will turn their mourning into gladness; I will give them comfort and joy instead of sorrow."

JEREMIAH 31:13

I n the midst of Israel's sorrow at their captivity by a pagan people, God promised a time of joy, when they would return to their land and be His people again. Are you separated from joy right now? Perhaps sin has overtaken your life, and you long to again lean close to God and share His tender love. Ask Him to turn your heart away from this barren landscape and return it to Him. Your sorrow can turn to joy.

The Kingdom of Heaven

Sorrowful, yet always rejoicing; poor, yet making many rich;
having nothing, and yet possessing everything.

2 CORINTHIANS 6:10

———

What a description of a Christian! Rejoicing in sorrow seems rather contradictory, doesn't it? How could the apostle Paul feel joy in such circumstances? Because God works in even less-than-perfect situations. In fact, He often works most powerfully when troubles load our plate. What do we have to rejoice in? The wonderful work God does in our lives, no matter what we face. We always possess the kingdom of heaven.

_____

_____

_____

_____

_____

_____

_____

_____

_____

_____

_____

_____

_____

_____

_____

_____

_____

_____

_____

_____

_____

_____

_____

_____

Praise God—No Matter What

The king will rejoice in God; all who swear by God's name will praise him.

PSALM 63:11

———

Need some joy in your life? Start praising God, and no matter what messy situations you face today, you'll begin rejoicing. Praise Him for who He is—His immense, loving nature that has blessed you so much. Thank Him for the love He has showered on you. As you remember His love, sorrow loses its grasp on your life.

Knowing God

Close to Jesus

"Be still, and know that I am God."

PSALM 46:10

———

So often, we seek to do things for God or to prove our Christian witness. But if we become simply caught up in busyness, we lose the distinction of our faith: a close relationship with Jesus. Knowing God is not about what we do, but about whom we love. Our good works mean little if we disconnect from Him. Spend time being still with God today, and a deepened knowledge of Him will be your blessing.

_____

_____

_____

_____

_____

_____

_____

_____

_____

_____

_____

_____

_____

_____

_____

_____

_____

_____

_____

_____

_____

_____

_____

God Is Great

I know that the LORD is great, that our LORD is greater than all gods.

PSALM 135:5

Other "gods" contend with Jesus in the marketplace of ideas, and devout Christians may encounter contention. But just as the psalmist recognized God's greatness, we can, too, as we look at the world around us. No other would-be deity shows forth its glory in creation. No other has provided His gracious salvation. If our Lord controls our lives, how can we look to any other gods?

Know Him Intimately

"I will take you as my own people, and I will be your God.
Then you will know that I am the LORD your God,
who brought you out from under the yoke of the Egyptians."

EXODUS 6:7

⸺◦◦◦⸺

God freed the Hebrews from slavery and brought them to their new land. But He didn't stop there. Today, He still proves Himself to people by freeing them from sin's slavery and creating loving relationships with them. Has God freed you from sin? Then know Him intimately. Draw near and enjoy His blessings, no matter what "slavery" you've faced before.

_____

_____

_____

_____

_____

_____

_____

_____

_____

_____

_____

_____

_____

_____

_____

_____

_____

_____

_____

_____

_____

_____

Father and Son

We know also that the Son of God has come and has given us understanding,
so that we may know him who is true. And we are in him who is true—even in his Son Jesus Christ.
He is the true God and eternal life.

1 JOHN 5:20

How do we know God? Through His Son, Jesus, who helps us understand the love of His Father. There is no space, no difference of opinion, between Father and Son. When we know the Son, we know God truly. Trust in one is trust in both.

Live Devotedly

Do you not know that you are the temple of God and that the Spirit of God dwells in you?

1 CORINTHIANS 3:16 NKJV

───

God lives within you, not in a distant place. When you act according to His Word, He acts. When you fail, people may begin to doubt Him. That's why Paul encourages you to live devotedly for your Lord. As one of His people, you're filled with His potent Spirit, who empowers you to live a holy life. Live in His strength always.

_____

_____

_____

_____

_____

_____

_____

_____

_____

_____

_____

_____

_____

_____

_____

_____

_____

_____

_____

_____

_____

_____

_____

Loving God

Perfecting Our Love

Jesus replied: " 'Love the Lord your God with all your heart and with all your soul and with all your mind.' "

MATTHEW 22:37

———

This simple command can be a real challenge, can't it? No matter how we try, in our own power, to love God completely, we always seem to fail somewhere. Only as God's Spirit works in our heart will our whole being become ever more faithful. God works in us day by day, perfecting our love. Ask Him to help you love Him today.

Love Is Action

Dear friends, let us love one another, for love comes from God.
Everyone who loves has been born of God and knows God.

1 JOHN 4:7

W ant to see love? Look at God. Seeking love in this world is bound to be confusing. But in our Lord, we see the clean, clear lines of real love—love we can share with our families, friends, and fellow believers. Love for our enemies. Love for our Savior. Apart from God, we cannot truly and sacrificially love others. Love isn't just a feeling, but the actions we take as we follow Him.

_____

_____

_____

_____

_____

_____

_____

_____

_____

_____

_____

_____

_____

_____

_____

_____

_____

_____

_____

_____

_____

_____

Seeing God

No one has seen God at any time. If we love one another,
God abides in us, and His love has been perfected in us.

1 JOHN 4:12 NKJV

H ow do we see God? Often, it's through other people. That's why it's important to have a com-passionate Christian witness—people see you and think God is like you if you claim His name. In that way, many people have gotten erroneous concepts about the Savior. But many more have come to love Him through faithful testimonies. Today, you can love others and show them clearly what Jesus looks like.

Gentle Reminder

If a man say, I love God, and hateth his brother, he is a liar:
for he that loveth not his brother whom he hath seen, how can he love God whom he hath not seen?

1 JOHN 4:20 KJV

———

John's letter surely challenges us. Now we wonder, *Do I love God at all?* Surely, on our own, we couldn't. But when we accept God and receive His love, our attitude changes. In Jesus, we can love even a bothersome brother. Sometimes we just need a gentle reminder.

_____

_____

_____

_____

_____

_____

_____

_____

_____

_____

_____

_____

_____

_____

_____

_____

_____

_____

_____

_____

_____

_____

_____

Sweet Sacrifice

Live a life of love, just as Christ loved us and gave himself up for us
as a fragrant offering and sacrifice to God.

EPHESIANS 5:2

—⊱∘⊰—

We don't think of sacrifice as being sweet. More often, we see it as hardship or drudgery. But when we have experienced the delightfulness of Jesus' sacrifice, which brought us into a love relationship with Him, we understand just what this verse means. Yet God calls us not only to receive love but to pass it on to others who also need to understand the sweetness of His sacrifice.

Learn from Jesus

"A new command I give you: Love one another.
As I have loved you, so you must love one another."

JOHN 13:34

How do we know how to love? We learn from Jesus. The Master had been with His disciples for three years when He spoke these words, and they had seen His love in action. We see it, too, in God's Word and in the lives of faithful believers. In His power, we can take what we know and follow Jesus, living out the words He spoke and the good examples we have seen.

$_____$

New Life

Looks Can Be Deceiving

Therefore we do not lose heart. Though outwardly we are wasting away,
yet inwardly we are being renewed day by day.

2 CORINTHIANS 4:16

On the outside, people see us getting older and frailer. But looks are deceiving. As Christians, we constantly build our belief, if we walk consistently with God. We're growing deeper in faith, being spiritually renewed every day. God's glory lies ahead of us, as on earth we learn to appreciate His love and compassion. Undaunted, we look ahead to eternity and a new body, made perfect by our Savior.

Life-Altering Impact

We were therefore buried with him through baptism into death in order that,
just as Christ was raised from the dead through the glory of the Father, we too may live a new life.

ROMANS 6:4

———ॐ———

Baptism is a picture of the old, sinful nature's death and the new faith-life God gives those who trust in Him. Belief in Jesus has a life-altering impact. One moment, a sinful person is dead, held in sin's grasp. The next, she becomes an entirely new person, alive in her Savior. Only Jesus offers this glorious freedom. Has He given it to you?

_____

_____

_____

_____

_____

_____

_____

_____

_____

_____

_____

_____

_____

_____

_____

_____

_____

_____

_____

_____

_____

_____

_____

Living in the Light

In him was life, and that life was the light of men.

JOHN 1:4

Jesus is a Christian's life and light, as anyone who has walked with Him for a while can tell you. Everything is different once He enters a soul. As a result, the new believer begins to make changes, cleaning out the dark corners of her existence so that the bright light shining within her will not fall on dirty places. She's living in the light, following Jesus.

New Life

Therefore, if anyone is in Christ, he is a new creation; old things have passed away; behold, all things have become new.

2 CORINTHIANS 5:17 NKJV

New life in Christ: What indescribable freedom to be separated from our sin! No longer bound by it but able to live in Him, we joyfully race into our new existence.

But in time, our tendency to fall into sin tarnishes God's gift. Suddenly we don't feel so new. "Old" Christians need only turn again to Christ for forgiveness, and the Spirit's cleansing makes us new again.

_____

_____

_____

_____

_____

_____

_____

_____

_____

_____

_____

_____

Celebrate Your Newness

If Christ is in you, the body is dead because of sin, but the Spirit is life because of righteousness.

ROMANS 8:10 NKJV

Know Jesus? Then your body and your fleshly desires are less important than your spirit. Because Jesus lives in you, sin has no permanent claim on your life. Though it tempts you and you may give in for a time, it no longer has a firm grasp on all your days. You can turn aside from it and dwell in your Lord instead. Celebrate your newness in Jesus: Live for Him today!

Obedience

You Are Valuable

Who can find a virtuous woman? for her price is far above rubies.

PROVERBS 31:10 KJV

Are you a virtuous woman? If so, you are truly valuable, no matter how unbelievers criticize you. Proverbs 31 says you can have a profitable life with good relationships, a happy home life, and successful business ventures, if you run your life according to God's principles. So don't worry about the opinions of others if they don't mesh with God's. Instead, obey Him and be a valuable jewel to your Lord.

_____

_____

_____

_____

_____

_____

_____

_____

_____

_____

_____

_____

_____

_____

_____

_____

_____

_____

_____

_____

_____

_____

Love and Obey

"Whoever has my commands and obeys them, he is the one who loves me."

JOHN 14:21

Do you feel you love God with all your heart? Then show it by obeying Him. Jesus paved the path for you. Through His own sacrificial life, He showed you what it means to obey the Father. A Christian who lives for herself, rather than God, shows wavering commitment. One who loves God wholeheartedly walks in Jesus' way, obeying His commands in scripture. Here is where we start: Love God? Then obey Him, too.

Blessings Will Come

"All these blessings shall come upon you and overtake you,
because you obey the voice of the Lord your God."

DEUTERONOMY 28:2 NKJV

———

Obey God; receive blessings. It seems simple enough, doesn't it? Then why do we obey and only get in more trouble than before? Perhaps it's because we're looking at it from our perspective, not His. Blessings do not always follow on the heels of obedience; they often take time to appear. Today's blessings may result from long-ago faithfulness. But because God has promised, we know good things will come, if only we wait.

_____

_____

_____

_____

_____

_____

_____

_____

_____

_____

_____

_____

_____

_____

_____

_____

_____

_____

_____

_____

_____

_____

_____

Into Eternity

Blessed are they that do his commandments, that they may have right to the tree of life,
and may enter in through the gates into the city.

REVELATION 22:14 KJV

The blessings of obedience not only impact us today; they follow us into eternity. Whatever we do to please God never dies. When we trust in Jesus, the works that demonstrate our faith give us joy now and remain secure for the future in the One who never changes. We look forward to life in the New Jerusalem even as we reap His blessings now.

Prayer

Brothers, pray for us.

1 THESSALONIANS 5:25

———

Do you find it hard to ask others to pray for you? Don't be afraid to take that step into humility. Paul wasn't when he asked the Thessalonians to pray for his ministry. Being part of the church requires an interdependence of prayers given and received. As members of a congregation pray for each other, their spirits connect in a new, caring way. Choose carefully those with whom you share private concerns, but never fear to ask a mature Christian to pray for you.

_____

_____

_____

_____

_____

_____

_____

_____

_____

_____

_____

_____

_____

_____

_____

_____

_____

_____

_____

_____

_____

_____

_____

_____

The Best Answer

Pray without ceasing.

1 THESSALONIANS 5:17 KJV

———

Haven't gotten an answer to your prayer? Don't give up. There's no time limit on speaking to God about your needs. It's just that we often work on a different time schedule than God. We want an answer yesterday, while He has something better in mind for tomorrow. So keep praying. God listens to His children and gives them the best answer, not the fastest one.

God Hears

"Therefore I tell you, whatever you ask for in prayer,
believe that you have received it, and it will be yours."

MARK 11:24

———∞———

This verse is not prescribing some magical incantation, but faith that God hears and answers our requests. When we trust that He knows our needs and wants to respond to them, we are in a position to receive. Would Jesus be proud of our requests? Do we seek the good of others? Or do we look only to our own desires? God answers prayers that reflect His will. How do yours stack up against this measure?

_____

_____

_____

_____

_____

_____

_____

_____

_____

_____

_____

_____

_____

_____

_____

_____

_____

_____

_____

_____

_____

_____

Turn to Him

Rejoicing in hope, patient in tribulation, continuing steadfastly in prayer.

ROMANS 12:12 NKJV

—∞—

When do you pray the most—in times of ease or trial? Like most folks, you probably bend God's ear when you're hurting physically or spiritually, and that makes sense. For who helps the way God does? Paul describes the Christian's best response to trouble in these pithy phrases. While the faithless might rail against God, complaining that He is unfair, Christians know otherwise. We have a hope, a reason for patience, and a Father who cares. Let's turn to Him, no matter what our need.

Love Your Enemy

"But I tell you: Love your enemies and pray for those who persecute you."

MATTHEW 5:44

Without God's strength, could any of us follow this command of Jesus for more than a very brief time? Consistently loving an enemy is a real challenge. If you hurt from pain inflicted by another, you hardly want to pray for her. But loving actions and prayer can bring great peace between two people at odds with each other. For those who consistently follow this command, strife may not last forever.

_____

_____

_____

_____

_____

_____

_____

_____

_____

_____

_____

Healing Power

The prayer of faith will save the sick, and the Lord will raise him up.
And if he has committed sins, he will be forgiven.

JAMES 5:15 NKJV

Have you seen the amazing healing power of prayer? As faithful Christians lift a sufferer up to God, He works in the body, but also in the heart and soul. Know someone who is ill? Pray for physical health to return. But don't forget to include spiritual needs, for the Great Physician treats the whole person. Some spiritual issue may be the real problem that requires healing.

Prayer from the Heart

Some trust in chariots, and some in horses;
but we will remember the name of the Lord our God.

———✦———

This may seem an odd prayer for a king going out to battle, but it shows where David's heart was. He knew his war equipment could fail, but God could not.

What danger can we face from which God is incapable of defending us? None. Where have we placed our trust—in Him or in worldly defenses?

_____

_____

_____

_____

_____

_____

_____

_____

_____

_____

_____

Repentance

Overcoming the Sin Barrier

Godly sorrow brings repentance that leads to salvation and leaves no regret.

2 CORINTHIANS 7:10

Godly sorrow comes when we feel the pain of our own sins. As we recognize our wrong-doing and know that our actions have hurt us, others, and even the heart of God, we reach the place to do something about it. We repent, and God offers His salvation.

Has sin come between you and your Savior? Turn at once in sorrow and ask Him to make everything right in your heart and soul. You'll never be sorry you did.

Cleansing Spirit

I came not to call the righteous, but sinners to repentance.

LUKE 5:32 KJV

———

Repentance isn't meant for "good people" who only have "tiny" sins to confess. This verse reminds us that no sin is too awful for God to hear about it. God calls all who are sinful—including those who have the most to fear from His awesome holiness. Each of us may hesitate to confess sins and admit to wrongs that embarrass us. But we are just the ones He calls. One moment of repentance, and His Spirit cleanses our lives.

_____

_____

_____

_____

_____

_____

_____

_____

_____

_____

_____

_____

Blessing behind Repentance

"Repent, then, and turn to God, so that your sins may be wiped out,
that times of refreshing may come from the Lord."

ACTS 3:19

⸺⸺

When we consider repentance, we tend to think it's hard. That's only because we're short-sighted. Giving up sin may not appeal to our hardened hearts because we're not looking at the blessing set behind repentance. Yet as we turn from sin, we feel the refreshing breath of God's Spirit bringing new life to our lives. Then does anything seem difficult?

Compassion to Others

"And if he sins against you seven times in a day, and seven times in a day returns to you, saying, 'I repent,' you shall forgive him."

LUKE 17:4 NKJV

———

When another offends us, do we pass on the forgiveness we have received? That's what Jesus commanded. Remembering how gracious God has been to us, we need to show graciousness to those who affront us, too. As we think of our many sins that God put behind His back, can we fail to show compassion to others?

———

———

———

———

———

———

———

———

———

———

———

———

———

_____

_____

_____

_____

_____

_____

_____

_____

_____

_____

_____

_____

Salvation

Available 24/7

"Blessed is the man to whom the LORD shall not impute sin."

ROMANS 4:8 NKJV

———

Sin forgiven: What a wonderful thought! No longer do we need to be dragged into wrongdoing, because God has cleansed our hearts. His Spirit sweeps through us, lifting the burden of sin from our lives. Though we still fail, in Christ, God will not hold the sin against us. Forgiveness, available 24/7, sends His Spirit through our lives again and again.

Reconcilers

God was reconciling the world to himself in Christ, not counting men's sins against them.
And he has committed to us the message of reconciliation.

2 CORINTHIANS 5:19

—⸺—

The Lord loved you so much that He paid a huge price to draw you into His arms. Jesus' sacrifice destroyed the sin barrier that separates humanity and God. Those who repent are reconciled to their holy God. But faith does not stop there. He makes us reconcilers, too, as He sends us out with the message that has meant so much: "God loves you, too."

_____

_____

_____

_____

_____

_____

_____

_____

_____

_____

_____

_____

_____

_____

_____

_____

_____

_____

_____

_____

_____

_____

_____

Saving Grace

My soul finds rest in God alone; my salvation comes from him.

PSALM 62:1

⸺

At the moment you repented of your sins and asked Jesus to control your life, God saved you. But He didn't stop there. Each day of your life, He continues His saving work. He redirects you, protects you, and provides for your every need. In any trouble, rest in Him. He will not fail.

Shine for Him

[Jesus] gave himself for us to redeem us from all wickedness
and to purify for himself a people that are his very own, eager to do what is good.

TITUS 2:14

Is there any sin from which Jesus cannot save us? No. As long as we look to Him, He will lead us into increasing, joyous holiness.

God takes sinful people and changes their lives, making them His hands in an evil world. As His people draw near to Him, putting off sin, their good works shine forth the nature of their Savior. Will you shine for Him today?

_____

_____

_____

_____

_____

_____

_____

_____

_____

_____

_____

_____

Our Partner

Continue to work out your salvation with fear and trembling.

PHILIPPIANS 2:12

———

Salvation is hard work! Not only did it require Jesus' crucifixion for our sins, but we have a part in the effort, too. We have to live out the commands in God's Word that make our faith have an impact on our world. But we need not feel discouraged, for we are not alone in the labor. God acts through us by His Spirit. What better working partner could we have than God Himself?

The Glory of Jesus

From the beginning God chose you to be saved. . . . He called you. . .that you might share in the glory of our Lord Jesus Christ.

2 THESSALONIANS 2:13–14

———

Did you know you share Jesus' glory? Not because you are doing a wonderful job as a Christian, but simply because He decided to call you to Himself. God chose to share Himself with you and make you like His Son. Daily, He calls you to learn more of His magnificence as you faithfully follow Him. Isn't it wonderful to share just a bit of God's greatness?

_____

_____

_____

_____

_____

_____

_____

_____

_____

_____

_____

Serving God

Spiritual Training

All Scripture. . .is useful for. . .training in righteousness,
so that the man of God may be thoroughly equipped for every good work.

2 TIMOTHY 3:16–17

Did you realize that God prepares you to do good works every day of your life? Because you believe in Him, He will lead you to do good, following His plan for your life.

How do you start? By reading the scriptures, His guidebook. There you will learn what to believe, how to act, and how to speak with love. Soon you'll be ready to put into action all you've learned.

Serving Others

You. . .were called to be free. But do not use your freedom to indulge the sinful nature;
rather, serve one another in love.

GALATIANS 5:13

———

As women, we know a lot about serving: We serve on many fronts and sometimes wonder why this is our lot. God tells us He freed us from sin, not to do what we like, but so we can share His love. If we're tempted to fulfill our own sinful desires, let's remind ourselves why we are here—we obey Jesus by doing good for others. If that's not our goal, we need redirection from Him.

_____

_____

_____

_____

_____

_____

_____

_____

_____

_____

_____

_____

_____

_____

_____

_____

_____

_____

_____

_____

_____

You're Equipped

You have been given fullness in Christ, who is the head over every power and authority.

COLOSSIANS 2:10

Do you feel incomplete or inadequate, unable to carry out the tasks God has given you? You aren't, you know, if you tap into His Spirit. God equips you to do all things in Him. If you feel overwhelmed, make sure you haven't taken on tasks rightfully belonging to someone else. God does not overload your life with busyness. He has a purpose for all you do. So be certain you're serving in the right place, doing the work He planned for you.

Make the Most

Since everything will be destroyed in this way, what kind of people ought you to be?
You ought to live holy and godly lives.

2 PETER 3:11

———

Knowing that the world will not last forever, how should we act? We have no devil-may-care option, in which we act as if eternity does not matter, because God calls us to live wholly for Him. The world's destruction should not make us careless but vigilant to make the most of our time. In the end, all we do here will not be lost but will pass on into eternity.

_____

_____

_____

_____

_____

_____

_____

_____

_____

_____

_____

_____

_____

_____

_____

_____

_____

_____

_____

_____

_____

_____

Spiritual Gifts

You Have Gifts!

Now to each one the manifestation of the Spirit is given for the common good.

1 CORINTHIANS 12:7

D id you know that you are a gifted person? God gives each of His children spiritual gifts designed to help themselves and others—wisdom, knowledge, faith, healing, to name just a few. As you grow spiritually, you begin to unwrap those presents from God. Over time, you may be surprised and blessed at how many He has provided for you.

Feeling unimportant? Remind yourself that you're gifted by God!

Grace Is a Gift

But unto every one of us is given grace according to the measure of the gift of Christ.

EPHESIANS 4:7 KJV

We don't usually think of grace as a "spiritual gift." But consider: It's the basis for all the gifts God gives us. Without His gracious forgiveness, we'd have nothing spiritually. Our sins so separate us that only His forgiveness allows us to approach Him. Whether we receive a large measure of grace or a smaller one, it is the perfect gift, given by Jesus, just for us. Let's appreciate what it cost Him and walk in Him today.

_____

_____

_____

_____

_____

_____

_____

_____

_____

_____

_____

_____

For His Glory

We have different gifts, according to the grace given us.

ROMANS 12:6

Your spiritual gifts are tailored especially for you. God has a purpose for your life. To help you accomplish it, He has given just the gifts you need—nothing more, nothing less. Doesn't knowing that God has gifted you in just the right way make you feel special? Thank Him for those gifts today, and use them for the glory of His kingdom and to help others.

Reach Out

Try to excel in gifts that build up the church.

1 CORINTHIANS 14:12

Paul's words to the Corinthians were meant for us, too. We should build up the church, not ourselves, through our spiritual gifts. When God gave you a special combination of spiritual abilities, it wasn't to make you feel important. He designed them to help you reach out to those who need to accept Him as Savior and to support other believers who share your mission to reach the world. Is that how you're using your gifts today?

_____

_____

_____

_____

_____

_____

_____

_____

_____

_____

_____

_____

_____

_____

_____

_____

_____

_____

_____

_____

_____

_____

Strength

In His Power

I can do all things through Christ who strengthens me.

PHILIPPIANS 4:13 NKJV

Need strength? Turn to God for all you need. Why take on life by yourself when He offers all you need? Often, as obedient Christians, we make great efforts with our feeble spiritual muscles. But ultimately, our own strength always fails. When Christ's Spirit works through us, the Christian life flows smoothly; in His power we accomplish His purposes. Today, is Christ bearing the burden, or are we? Only He has the might we need in our lives.

Christian Strength

Finally, be strong in the Lord and in his mighty power.

EPHESIANS 6:10

When you rely on God's strength, what are you tapping into? Not some small pool of power that fails at a critical moment. The Christian's strength is mighty, because God is mighty. He who created the universe does not have a short arm that cannot reach down to your situation. Shining stars testify to His authority. Galaxies in space are ordered by His hand. Can He not order your life, too? Ask Him to use His strength in your life, and you will have all you need.

_____

_____

_____

_____

_____

_____

_____

_____

_____

_____

_____

Have Courage

Be on your guard; stand firm in the faith; be men of courage; be strong.

1 CORINTHIANS 16:13

———

Being a Christian can take lots of courage. As the world around us becomes increasingly hostile to God and our personal lives become tense because of our beliefs, we feel the challenge. But we are not defenseless. Christians through the ages have faced these troubles and triumphed. The Lord who supported them gives us strength, too. Let us stand fast for Jesus, calling on His Spirit to strengthen our lives. Then we will be strong indeed.

Uplift Others

We who are strong ought to bear with the failings of the weak and not to please ourselves.

So God has made you strong in some area—perhaps by experience, as you have struggled to obey Him. Now, how do you respond to others? Don't criticize those who have different experiences or other strengths, or carp about the failings of new, weak Christians. Instead, use your power to uplift others. Come alongside and help. Then God's strength will have helped you both.

_____

_____

_____

_____

_____

_____

_____

_____

_____

_____

_____

Seek His Strength

Our sufficiency is from God.

2 CORINTHIANS 3:5 NKJV

———

Feel unable to take on life? Paul knows how you feel. He didn't see himself as the perfect apostle we often imagine he was. Knowing his own flaws and failures, Paul recognized the work Jesus did in him every day. God made His servant sufficient to his tasks. He'll do it for you, too, as you walk in faith and seek His strength.

Success

You Will Prosper

"But you shall meditate in it [the Book of the Law] day and night. . . . Do not turn from it. . .that you may prosper."

JOSHUA 1:7–8 NKJV

God promised success to Joshua if he obeyed His Word. That promise works for you, too. But sometimes you may not feel that obeying God has brought you great prosperity. Just wait. It may take time, the success may not take the form you expect, or you may not see the results until you reach heaven, but God will prosper those who do His will. He promised it, and His promises never fail.

_____

_____

_____

_____

_____

_____

_____

_____

_____

_____

_____

_____

_____

_____

_____

_____

_____

_____

_____

_____

_____

_____

_____

Eternal Blessings

A faithful man will abound with blessings, but he who hastens to be rich will not go unpunished.

PROVERBS 28:20 NKJV

Faithfulness to God or success in the world: Have you had to choose between them? Seeking the world's goals brings short-term benefits, but only God provides abundant and ongoing blessings for those who put serving Him first in their lives. Though worldly blessings last for a day, a year, or a few years, they cannot remain for eternity. When you consider success, think of the kind that really lasts.

Living in Him

The meek will inherit the land and enjoy great peace.

PSALM 37:11

⸻

You might call this God's definition of success: a profitable land that provides for His people and His peace that provides a blessed life. Notice that money and other possessions aren't mentioned. But the peace of living in Him flows freely to those who abide in Him. Would this be success to you? If not, what does that tell you about your spiritual life?

_____

_____

_____

_____

_____

_____

_____

_____

_____

_____

_____

_____

_____

_____

_____

_____

_____

_____

_____

_____

_____

_____

Real Success

Save now, we beseech You, O Lord; send now prosperity,
O Lord, we beseech You, and give to us success!

PSALM 118:25 AMP

Is it wrong to pray for success? No. But notice that the Bible connects success to God's salvation. Prosperity or any other achievement means little when it's separated from God's will and our obedience to Him. When you ask to attain something, do you also seek God's saving grace in that part of your life? If so, you'll have real success—spiritual and temporal blessings.

Temptation

Escape Hatch

No temptation has seized you except what is common to man. And God is faithful. . . . When you are tempted, he will also provide a way out so that you can stand up under it.

1 CORINTHIANS 10:13

———

No matter how powerful it seems, you need not give in to temptation. God always provides you with an escape hatch. When temptation pulls at you, turn your eyes to Jesus. Replace that tempting object with Him, and you will not fall.

_____

_____

_____

_____

_____

_____

_____

_____

_____

_____

_____

_____

_____

_____

_____

_____

_____

_____

_____

_____

_____

_____

_____

Ask Jesus

Because he himself suffered when he was tempted, he is able to help those who are being tempted.

Hebrews 2:18

———

Why can Jesus help us when temptation strikes? Because He has walked a mile in our shoes. He knows how strongly sin attracts us. But because He never fell prey to it, He can effectively show us how to resist even the strongest enticement. The biggest mistakes we make are not calling on Him and not persistently seeking His powerful aid when Satan repeatedly lures us into sin. Need help? Just ask Jesus.

Lean on Jesus

"Therefore if the Son makes you free, you shall be free indeed."

JOHN 8:36 NKJV

Sometimes we don't feel freed from sin. Temptations draw us, even though we love Jesus. So His words here can be both comforting and challenging. The Jews wanted to trust in their spiritual history, not God. That plan didn't work well for them, and it won't work for us, either. We can't rely on history or our past deeds to put sin behind us. What will work? Leaning on Jesus every day, trusting Him to make us free indeed!

_____

_____

_____

_____

_____

_____

_____

_____

_____

_____

_____

God Is Greater

Each one is tempted when, by his own evil desire, he is dragged away and enticed.

JAMES 1:14

———

God does not draw us into temptation. He is holy, unable to tempt anyone into wrongdoing. The attraction to sin comes from within us, because our evil desires lead us toward sin. When we face situations that encourage our own wickedness, they are not designed by God to make us fall. Instead, they provide opportunities to turn to Him and progressively turn away from iniquity. No evil within us is so great that God is not greater still.

God's Protection

The Lord knows how to deliver the godly out of temptations
and to reserve the unjust under punishment for the day of judgment.

2 PETER 2:9 NKJV

Feeling surrounded by temptations? God hasn't forgotten you. He knows how to protect His children from harm and offers His wisdom to His children. Maybe you need to avoid places that could lead you into sin—that may mean taking an action such as finding a new job or new friends. When God is trying to protect you, don't resist. Sin is never better than knowing Him.

_____

_____

_____

_____

_____

_____

_____

_____

_____

_____

_____

Thankfulness

Give Thanks

Give thanks to the God of gods. His love endures forever.

PSALM 136:2

Having trouble being thankful? Read Psalm 136. You'll be reminded of the wonders of God's power and His enduring love. The God who protected Israel watches over you, too. Even when there may be little in your life to rejoice about, you can always delight in Him. Give thanks to God. He has not forgotten you—His love endures forever.

God Saves

I will give you thanks, for you answered me; you have become my salvation.

Psalm 118:21

———

A new believer didn't write this verse. The psalmist thanks God not just for loving him enough to tear him from the claws of original sin; instead, this mature man of faith recognizes that God saves him every day, whenever he is in trouble. God does this in your life, too. What salvation has He worked in your life recently? What thanks do you need to offer Him now?

_____

_____

_____

_____

_____

_____

_____

_____

_____

_____

_____

_____

Eternal Appreciation

O Lord my God, I will give you thanks forever.

PSALM 30:12

———

Even in eternity, you will be thanking God. The appreciation of God's mercy by His people never stops. Without His grace, we would be forever separated from Him, lost in the cares of sin and a hellish existence. The bliss of a heavenly eternity could not be our inheritance.

Could you thank Jesus too much now? Or could you ever find enough words to show Him your love? Maybe it's time to get started on your eternal appreciation of your Lord.

Appreciation Overflow

Continue to live in [Jesus], rooted and built up in him, strengthened in the faith as you were taught, and overflowing with thankfulness.

Colossians 2:6–7

Strong Christians are thankful Christians. As we realize all Jesus has sacrificed for us and appreciate our inability to live the Christian life on our own, we remember to praise our Savior for His grace. Today, we can be rooted in Jesus, strong in our faith, and thankful to the One who has given us these blessings. Let's overflow with appreciation!

_____

_____

_____

_____

_____

_____

_____

_____

_____

_____

_____

_____

Wonderful Thanks

*Oh, give thanks to the L*ORD*, for He is good! For His mercy endures forever.*

PSALM 136:1 NKJV

———

Now, honestly, how do you respond to this call for thanks? Does your heart leap at the opportunity, or does this exhortation just hit you with a dull thud? Why is it so important to thank God? Because He will always be merciful to you. Whether you rejoice easily or hit the floor with a thud, if you have trusted in the Savior, He still loves you. Isn't that something wonderful to give thanks for?

Troubles

God Calls Us to Joy

Consider it pure joy, my brothers, whenever you face trials of many kinds.

JAMES 1:2

———⊷———

Joy? To be faced with trials should cause us joy? Hard to imagine, isn't it? But God calls us to joy when unbelievers persecute us because of our faith or when our situation is merely difficult. It is a joy to Him that we have stood firm in faith, and He calls us to share His delight. That doesn't mean we seek out trials but that we face the situation hand in hand with God. In trials, our spiritual strength increases.

_____

_____

_____

_____

_____

_____

_____

_____

_____

_____

_____

_____

Look Ahead to Heaven

For our light and momentary troubles are achieving for us an eternal glory that far outweighs them all.

2 CORINTHIANS 4:17

W hat trouble could you face on earth that will not seem small in heaven? No pain from this life will impede you there. Blessing for faithful service to God will replace each heartache that discourages you today. When trials and troubles beset you, look ahead to heaven. Jesus promises you an eternal reward if you keep your eyes on Him.

Joy Is Straight Ahead

The genuineness of your faith, being much more precious than gold that perishes,
though it is tested by fire, may be found to praise, honor, and glory at the revelation of Jesus Christ.

1 PETER 1:7 NKJV

Trials have a purpose in our lives. As a smith heats up gold to purify it, God heats up our lives to make spiritual impurities rise to the surface. If we cooperate with Him, sin is skimmed off our lives, purifying our faith. Cleansed lives bring glory to God and joy to us. If a trial lies before you today, envision the joy ahead.

_____

_____

_____

_____

_____

_____

_____

_____

_____

_____

_____

_____

_____

_____

_____

_____

_____

_____

_____

_____

_____

_____

_____

_____

Hope in God Alone

Because of the LORD's great love we are not consumed, for his compassions never fail.

LAMENTATIONS 3:22

⸺⸹⸺

Despite his deep troubles, as Jeremiah sorrowed over Judah's exile, hope remained in his heart. Though he and his nation faced terrible trials, the prophet understood that God would still uphold them. God's compassion never fails His hurting people.

No matter how we struggle, we share the prophet's hope. God alone comforts our hearts as we stumble along a rocky trail.

His Concern

The righteous cry out, and the LORD hears, and delivers them out of all their troubles.

PSALM 34:17 NKJV

As God's child, you have His ear 24/7, if only you will pray. Every need, trouble, or praise is His concern. And not only will He hear about your trials, but He will deliver you from them. Feel discouraged in your troubles? You need not stay that way. Just spend time with Jesus. His help is on the way.

_____

_____

_____

_____

_____

_____

_____

_____

_____

_____

_____

_____

_____

Wisdom

Wisdom in God

Wisdom is the principal thing; therefore get wisdom: and with all thy getting get understanding.

PROVERBS 4:7 KJV

Have you ever thought of yourself as wise? The Bible says you can be. You don't need a lot of education or a certain IQ. Real wisdom is found in God. Simply obey your Lord's commandments and make knowing Him well your first priority. Seek after wisdom, and you will find it in Him. As you daily search for truth in the Word, your understanding grows.

Greater Ways

For since, in the wisdom of God, the world through wisdom did not know God,
it pleased God through the foolishness of the message preached to save those who believe.

1 CORINTHIANS 1:21 NKJV

To this world, God's wisdom doesn't look very wise. Anyone who denies Jesus is blind to the depth of insight God showed in sending His Son to die for us and then raising Him from the dead. But those who accept His sacrifice understand that God's ways are greater than ours and His astuteness far outweighs our own. As His wisdom fills our once-foolish lives, we gain a new perspective on His perception.

_____

_____

_____

_____

_____

_____

_____

_____

_____

_____

_____

_____

Wise Humility

Woe unto them that are wise in their own eyes, and prudent in their own sight!

Isaiah 5:21 KJV

———

Wisdom without humility isn't wisdom at all. When we feel astute under our own power, we are actually in big trouble and are heading into foolishness! The truly wise person recognizes that all wisdom comes from God, not frail humans. As we tap into His mind and connect with His astuteness, we are wise indeed. No one is wiser than God.

Wise Words

She speaks with wisdom, and faithful instruction is on her tongue.

PROVERBS 31:26

The virtuous woman's mouth speaks kindly wisdom. Hers is no sharp tongue that destroys relationships. As we seek to do God's will, truthful yet caring speech must be ours. Wise words heal hurting hearts. If we have trouble knowing what words bring God's healing, we need only to ask Him to let His Spirit bring wisdom and kindness to our tongues. When we speak as His Spirit directs, we are wise indeed.

_____

_____

_____

_____

_____

_____

_____

_____

_____

_____

_____

_____

_____

_____

_____

_____

_____

_____

_____

_____

_____

Seek Counsel

The way of a fool is right in his own eyes, but he who heeds counsel is wise.

PROVERBS 12:15 NKJV

Listening to others who are wise brings us wisdom, too. Before we make serious choices, we need to seek the counsel of others. How can we recognize the wise ones? Those who have experience and faith and who have made decisions that blessed their lives can pass their wisdom on to us, too. Is there some wise person you need to consult now?

Witness

Shine On

"You are the light of the world. A city on a hill cannot be hidden."

MATTHEW 5:14

———⊶⊷———

God means you to be a light set where the world can see it clearly—not a hidden flame behind closed doors, with curtains drawn. Being a light isn't always easy—people see everything you do, and they don't always like it. Don't let the critics stop you. Your works were ordained to glorify God, not to make people comfortable. Knowing that, are you ready to shine today?

_____

_____

_____

_____

_____

_____

_____

_____

_____

_____

_____

_____

_____

_____

_____

_____

_____

_____

_____

_____

_____

_____

_____

Share His Love

I pray that you may be active in sharing your faith,
so that you will have a full understanding of every good thing we have in Christ.

PHILEMON 1:6

M any of us have a hard time sharing our faith. So when we hear Paul's encouragement to Philemon, our hearts lift, knowing we aren't the only ones who struggle. Isn't the challenge of witnessing to others worth it, once we've read this promise? The salvation of others and our own appreciation of our Lord: Could we have better reasons to share His love?

Kind Words

Let your speech always be with grace, seasoned with salt,
that you may know how you ought to answer each one.

COLOSSIANS 4:6 NKJV

Your words are a vital part of your witness. Speak to an unbeliever ungraciously, and chances are good that she will never forget it. But study and grow in the Word; then speak wisely and generously to others, and God can use your words to win them to His kingdom. People respond well to kindness and flavorful speech. What are your words saying today?

_____

_____

_____

_____

_____

_____

_____

_____

_____

_____

_____

_____

Turn from Wrong

There is therefore now no condemnation to those who are in Christ Jesus,
who do not walk according to the flesh, but according to the Spirit.

ROMANS 8:1 NKJV

No condemnation! What a wonderful thought for sinners! Forgiven, we know the comfort of having heaven as our ultimate destination. But have we also read the second part of the verse? This is no blanket agreement that okays sin. The joy of our freedom must lead us to turn from all wrong. Our Lord gives the strength to grow in Him.

God's Compassionate Salvation

Do not repay anyone evil for evil. Be careful to do what is right in the eyes of everybody.

ROMANS 12:17

Tit-for-tat retribution for evil is not a principle of our compassionate God. We understand this if we've received His undeserved salvation. With such a gift, God has opened our hearts to treating our enemies as He has treated us. If we refuse to count up each wrong and repay it with harshness, lost souls may understand God's compassionate salvation. By doing right, even when we receive wrong in return, we become powerful witnesses.

_____

_____

_____

_____

_____

_____

_____

_____

_____

_____

_____

Live Out Forgiveness

Be kind and compassionate to one another, forgiving each other, just as in Christ God forgave you.

EPHESIANS 4:32

———

Because all Christians are forgiven sinners, not perfect people, the need for forgiveness does not stop at the church door. So Paul calls us to live out compassion not only to the world but within our congregations, as well. As we set aside anger and other harsh attitudes, we live out the forgiveness all believers have received. Is there any better way to share His love?

Work

Inheritors of Earth

"Blessed are the meek, for they will inherit the earth."

Matthew 5:5

In the workplace, meekness isn't often seen as a positive thing. "Looking out for number one" is the theory of many who tout assertiveness as the way to get the most out of life.

But God doesn't say that. Ultimately, those who follow Him faithfully and show their belief to the world will not be the "nice guys" who "finish last," but the inheritors of this earth. What plot of earth might God have mapped out for you?

_____

_____

_____

_____

_____

_____

_____

_____

_____

_____

_____

_____

_____

_____

_____

_____

_____

_____

_____

_____

_____

_____

Everything for God

Whatever you do, work at it with all your heart, as working for the Lord.

COLOSSIANS 3:23

⸺❦⸺

Did you know you are not really working for your boss? Yes, you report to the one whom your company hired in that position, but ultimately, you do everything for God, not a man or woman. So even if your boss isn't great to work for, remind yourself that you are accountable to Jesus. No matter who has the position above yours, your Lord is always in charge of your future.

Serious Business

Make it your ambition to lead a quiet life, to mind your own business and to work with your hands.

1 Thessalonians 4:11

Whether we work at a computer or on a factory production line, those of us who work with our hands shouldn't feel unimportant. Manual labor is serious business in God's sight. Christians who quietly, faithfully go about their business day by day make an important contribution, bearing God's message to a wide range of people. What a testimony our lives become when we live out this verse.

_____

_____

_____

_____

_____

_____

_____

_____

_____

_____

_____

God's Favor

May the favor of the Lord our God rest upon us; establish the work of our hands for us.

PSALM 90:17

━━━━━

Want your work to be effective? Don't make sure the boss knows every good thing you do. Seek God's favor, and He will see to it that your work really gets the job done, whether you're caring for a child, arguing a legal case, or waiting on a customer. Our Lord makes His people productive for Him as they serve others in His name.

Worldliness

No Compromises

Do not love the world or anything in the world. If anyone loves the world,
the love of the Father is not in him.

1 JOHN 2:15

———

This verse is likely to hit us right where we live. The world's way tempts us more than we'd like to admit. But when we feel the pull of worldliness, do we remember that we're actually making a larger decision about loving God? Gaining the small, temporal things is not worth compromising our faith. Let's save our love for the One who really deserves it.

_____

_____

_____

_____

_____

_____

_____

_____

_____

_____

_____

_____

_____

_____

_____

_____

_____

_____

_____

_____

_____

_____

_____

More Than Temporary

Do not be afraid when one becomes rich, when the glory of his house is increased;
for when he dies he shall carry nothing away; his glory shall not descend after him.

PSALM 49:16–17 NKJV

T his is the Bible's way of saying, "You can't take it with you." When life ends, the only treasures that remain are the works we have done for Jesus. Money and fame cling to earth, soon to be forgotten. So when unbelievers seem to get all the goodies, we just remember that the treasures we send ahead to heaven are greater than any temporary gain.

Belong to Jesus

"If you belonged to the world, it would love you as its own. As it is, you do not belong to the world, but I have chosen you out of the world. That is why the world hates you."

JOHN 15:19

—⟨≈⟩—

Don't expect the world to love you for loving Jesus. Because He doesn't accept its evil, and neither do you, the world is at enmity with both of you. That's not such a bad thing. To whom would you rather belong: Jesus, who holds eternity's joys in His hands, or the world, which offers so much sin and pain?

_____

_____

_____

_____

_____

_____

_____

_____

_____

_____

_____

_____

_____

_____

_____

_____

_____

_____

_____

_____

_____

_____

Kingdom-Purposed Friendship

"I tell you, use worldly wealth to gain friends for yourselves, so that when it is gone,
you will be welcomed into eternal dwellings."

LUKE 16:9

There is a good way to use the things of the world, and Jesus describes it here. God has given us wealth to share with others, making use of it to further God's kingdom. Though we may not have more than a pot of soup and some bread to offer, they can be the start of a kingdom-purposed friendship. What do you have that God can use this way?

Scripture Index

OLD TESTAMENT

Proverbs

Ecclesiastes

Isaiah

Jeremiah

NEW TESTAMENT